I0560784

IN THE
COVENANT
OF THE
ARK
A PROPHETIC JOURNEY OF HOPE

Judith Perrine Armour

Olympus Story House

Table of Contents

To Father Odo Recker, OSB—formerly Father
Carl Recker, Diocese of Toledo, Ohio

Acknowledgments

I am most grateful to my husband, Jim, who never, for a moment, doubted the voice of the Lord in my life. He stood by my side in all things with his love and guidance and cooperated with God's plan every step of the way.

I celebrate each of my children, Patrick, Kevin, Katie, and Ryan, who are amazing kids. They created enough chaos to keep me grounded and demonstrated patience as we navigated the difficult times of our trials.

This journey could never have occurred except for the guidance and spiritual direction from Father Carl Recker, who was the liaison for the Charismatic Renewal in the Toledo Diocese. Father is now the vocational director at Mount Angel Abbey and Seminary in Oregon and is now known as Father Odo Recker, OSB. He, along with Rev. George Koerber, Rev. James Bacik, Friar Kieren Kay, OSB Conv., Father Samuel Houser, and Rev. William Sullivan, were all holy priests who supported our ministries and ongoing contemplative formation. I particularly thank Bishop James Hoffman for the initial generosity and spiritual support he gave to the start-up of the Open Door Ministry and the blessings he gave to the healing team. It is my prayer that other priests and bishops will take their example of prayer and discernment for God's action in the lives of the laity.

INTRODUCTION

There is a storm brewing that is dividing us and others around the world from the very core of who we are called to be as individuals, as countries, and as religions. This noise is creating chaos with a din that no one seems to be able to break through to bring forth truth and hope. We are divided in politics, race, income, social norms, and ethnicity. Politicians, bobbleheads on news programs, and media stars would try to convince you of what you should believe. They have wealth, power, and adulation, yet many have lives that are a travesty of dysfunction.

Stop! Put down your cell phones and your iPads, and turn off the computers. It is time to silence your lives and look within the core of your being to find love, healing, and the path to a world at peace. It is time to listen! The prophet Joel tells us:

> *And it shall come to pass afterward,*
> *That I will pour out my spirit on all flesh;*
> *your sons and daughters shall prophesy, your old men*
> *shall dream dreams,*
> *and your young men will see visions.*
> *Even upon the menservants and maidservants*
> *In those days, I will pour out my spirit. (Joel 3:1–3)*

Could the time that the prophet Joel talks about be upon us?

Certainly, the psyche of the people's lives today is not much different from those in biblical times of Joel. If God is trying to talk to our hearts, how do we listen? First, we must learn to be silent. Let me share a page of my journal on a reflection of silence:

I don't know when I first embraced the silence or entered into its wake. Caught in its current, it carried me into uncharted waters of the unconscious. Spiraling ever deeper throughout my life, into the solitude, there I found the dance. A consuming turn of passion that changes the direction of our lives. Like the tide, we are drawn by forces unseen.

In the abyss of this travel, we lose our sense and our senses. Then we become blended into an illumination. The cacophony of sounds that disordered our lives are silenced by the stillness; a sweet melody, a lover's dance, a fragrance of mystery, a taste of honey. There, transcendent love meets us. God speaks.

Gradually, we ebb like the tide and are brought back to shore. Once again, grounded in reality, we return from this journey, inexplicitly changed. How and to what extent cannot be measured in the moment. It will be played out in time. Therein, all things are transformed.

Through the sharing that takes place in these pages, may you, too, find a God who listens, a God who speaks, and a God who heals. He desires that each one of us be able to live life to its fullness, to find peace and happiness in knowing that we are loved beyond measure. He wants us to accept our failings, to look to the care of others, to seek truth, and, most of all, to unite us in faith and charity to one another. God calls us to be living stones, the foundation for his kingdom on earth.

We must abandon the premise of popular culture that we do not have time for God and that he may or may not exist. There are those who tell us that it is politically incorrect to mention God in public forums, whether in word or symbol. To move away from our Judeo-Christian foundation and to deny God's existence is to move us closer to destruction. We will become blind to the beauty of all creation and to all that God has planned for us. Let us begin to believe in the power of prayer to bring about the impossible in this world. May we begin at the beginning with a mustard seed of faith and the innocence of a child to be able to see with new eyes and hear with new ears all that is possible with a God who loves us.

Now, sit quietly, breathe in and out slowly, shed the distractions of the world, and focus only on the one being, who is our God.

CHAPTER 1
The Call

Here I am, Lord
Is it I, Lord?
I have heard you calling in the night
I will go, Lord
If you lead me
I will hold your people in my heart.
—"Here I am Lord" by Dan Schutte, 1979
(based on Isaiah 6:8 and 1 Samuel 3:4)

It would seem impossible for me to share the full scope of this journey into the mystical with the general audience of people who have little time for anything spiritual. Not to mention many of the younger generation, who scoff at religion and find it hard to define the spiritual or to give a name to God. However, I invite you into my life so that I can bear witness to the fact that God is real. He is an awesome and omnipotent being, who will reach beyond time and space to bring us into a fourth dimension of life where *"eye has not seen, and ear has not heard, and what has not entered, the human heart, what God has prepared for those who love him"* (1 Corinthians 2:9).

I do not know when I first found my friendship with silence, but I am comfortable in this void. Nothing in my dreams or imaginings would prepare me for the day that my God would choose to visit me in this quiet. His whisper was like a quake that shook me loose from my complacency and rattled the core of my being. It redefined who I was to become.

It all began with the asking, "Who am I, and is this all there is to life?" I was thirty-five at the time, happily married to my loving husband Jim, mother of two sons, and an accomplished research chemist. I had traveled extensively and lived a life of privilege and good health. On the outside, I had all that one would want in life. Yet there was a deep sense of longing to find the peace that would put the fragments of who I was into perspective. So my prayer began: "God, show me what is missing from my life!"

I repeated this prayer daily, in between trying to keep up with the activities of two active sons, a part-time job at a medical college, and volunteer work in my community. One night, in my exhaustion, I fell asleep in the middle of my nighttime prayer, only to be awakened by a physical jolt and a bright light. I was startled awake and thought that perhaps the house had been struck by lightning. When I got out of bed, I noticed it was a clear night, and there needed to be another explanation. Then I thought, *Could it be the electric blanket meeting its demise?* I crawled on the floor and saw that it wasn't even plugged in.

I got back into bed and lay quiet when I heard an inner voice say, "*You have been baptized in the Holy Spirit.*" My immediate response was that I had some sort of epileptic seizure, and now, I was having a psychotic episode. My prayer changed to: "Dear God, please do not let me go crazy thinking that I hear your voice."

Little did I expect the response: "*Why do you doubt me?*"

Me: "Well, if that is you, God, why me?"

He responded: "*Because even as a child, you had great faith.*"

As this dialogue progressed, I was shown the sadness and fears of my childhood and the times I prayed for help. The Lord showed me every instance and every prayer I prayed and how he answered them. In the days and nights to follow, I was shown more and more of my life as I drowned in tears—both from the sadness of my memories and the omnipotent love that I was shown by God, who never left my side in my darkest moments. God showed me how he answered those prayers with the people that he placed in my life and the spiritual awareness of the strength and courage that I gained through prayer. The broken child was being healed! Like an onion, layers and layers of fear, abandonment, self-loathing, and guilt were lifted from me. My dreams were no longer the common nightmares held over from my childhood, but those very nightmares were now turned into beautiful, fulfilling dreams with exhilarating conclusions. Indeed, our dreams are God's hidden language. Today, dreams, along with my prayer, still play an important part in my self-awareness and the balance in my life. They bring me back into focus and peace.

As my healing continued, I was awakened one night in that place between sleep and wakefulness, a state of awareness that is still unconscious, a place of detachment from the mortal realm. I saw in a vision what looked like burning words; it was through my questioning that God led me to his Holy Scripture. He told me to open the Bible and I would see his purpose. There I found the verse previously referenced from 1 Corinthians 2:9–10.

That same night, I found myself at the Pentecost, Acts 2:1–41, when Jesus's apostles were anointed with the Holy Spirit in the form of tongues of fire. The apostles began to speak in other languages and were anointed with the power to spread the Good News of Christ throughout the world. I was led to Paul's letters in 1 Corinthians 12:1–11. In these passages, the charismatic gifts of the Holy Spirit are presented: the gifts of wisdom and knowledge, faith, healing, miraculous powers, prophecy, and the power to distinguish one spirit from another, the gifts of tongues, and the interpretation of tongues.

When I asked the Lord which of these gifts I was given, he responded that I had received all of them, but the greatest of my gifts was discernment. I had yet to understand what this would mean for me and for others open to God's grace. Flowing from God's love, we all have these gifts within us. We can choose to acknowledge these gifts, surrender to God, and ask for his guidance, then God will use us. This Ruah, the spirit or breath of God, is the same spirit that was given to all of us when God created us in his image. Before we were born, he called us by name and knitted us in our mother's womb (Jeremiah 1:5). This is the spirit of God, who will one day unite us all as one family in faith. The Lord said, *"No one will compromise what they believe in their faith, they will only have to build on it."*

I took all of these "spiritual visits" into my heart to reflect on them. I had yet to reveal to anyone what I was experiencing. My religious formation never mentioned that a normal individual could hear the voice of God speaking to their heart. I assumed that if I were to reveal myself to anyone, they would think that I had experienced psychotic events. I continued to pray and soon found that my favorite prayer of the rosary had now turned to tongues—a beautiful expression of prayer that sounds foreign and can be sung in angelic melodies. (Truly a gift for, if you ever sat around me in church, you would know that I have the worst singing voice, and only earplugs will spare you.)

It was a dream that finely led me to seek out a priest.

In the dream, I was being called away from a wedding and found that the white gown of the wedding was covered in blood. I was led to a tragic event, where people seemed to be severely injured and dying in the streets that were on fire. As I prayed for them, they were being healed. I then took the children by the hand and led them across a narrow, isthmus-like landmass, away from the chaos and death in the city. We followed a star. Several children were not focused and were falling into what seemed like an abyss. I had to yell to keep them safe as we were led into a desert. We wandered in the desert as we were buffeted by strong winds, and we finally came to the ocean, where a boat was waiting for us. It had a sail on it, but once we all got into the boat, a large wave came and tore off the sail, and we were lifted to the crest of another huge wave. I then realized that the boat had become an ark. When the ocean settled, we saw through the calm, the rainbow in the sky.

I awoke from the dream into an altered state of consciousness between waking and dreaming when I heard the Lord say:

Now, I will explain the dream. I have called you to leave the celebration of life as you know it and come follow me. By the blood of my salvation, I will heal my children. I ask you to gather my children of every nation, race, and creed, who are dying in their hearts, their minds, and in their souls. Tell them to trust me to heal them. I will lead them to safety. The path to me is narrow, but if you keep your eye on "Jesus, the Morning Star," my Spirit will guide you. There are many who will stray and try to rob you of what is mine, but you must admonish them like a loving father and tell them to turn away from their sin. The barrenness of this world can no longer nurture my children. I will lead them into the desert, where the winds of change will wipe clean the face of the earth. I will lead them into my ark, two by two, those from every nation, every race, and every creed. While the sails and masts may be torn down, my children will find themselves safe in the hull of my ark, which is the foundation of my church. I will cast them high above the water, which is the waters of baptism. I promise to them the same covenant that I gave to Noah; they will not be destroyed. This is the covenant of my ark, my mother, and my church.

The Lord followed this by saying, *"In order that you know this is true, open the Scripture, and you will open to the page where I was welcomed into Jerusalem by the laying of the palms. As I was welcomed then, so you welcome me now."*

This indeed proved to be true; a random opening of the Bible led me to the passage in John 12:12–13, where Jesus was welcomed into Jerusalem by the laying of the palms.

The Lord followed up by saying, *"However, I warn you that the devil knew of these gifts before you did, and now, remember back to one who sold them for profit."* This taught me the reality of evil; for it was easy to recall an experience five years prior to this time when I found myself in the presence of a mind reader, who the corporation my husband worked for had hired to be an entertainment at a convention. For two days, I could not stand to be in the same room with this man. I experienced a hatred coming from him that was a blasphemy directed at me through an ESP-like experience. It consumed my every thought. It became a physical and visible affront to my mind as blasphemies were projected on the walls. At the time, I chastised myself for falling prey to the power of suggestion that this man could read my thoughts and project an image on my mind. I prayed ardently that the power of my intellect could overcome this experience. I called upon the name of Jesus repeatedly like a mantra. The blasphemy stopped. The next day, the gentleman brought a woman along, and both seemed to be uncomfortable in my presence while the previous day, he was ego-driven in his conversations. I learned then of the extraordinary power in the name of Jesus! This individual then asked me who I was and what I did for a living! My response was that "I was a wife and mother who knew Christ."

Now that I knew the devil had my number, I was in desperate need of a priest and a spiritual director. God blessed me in this search as I started with my pastor, who said, "I believe that this is an authentic religious experience since I know you and I know the fruits of your life. I am therefore recommending that you seek out Father Carl Recker, who is a Jungian spiritual director and liaison for the Charismatic Renewal to the Bishop." My pastor also recommended a mystical theologian, whom I met with many years later, Father

James Bacik. Father Carl was able to laugh with me, teach me, and mentor me as my spiritual director for over five years. Without his guidance and trust in God's actions in my life, I would not have been able to cooperate with God's plans for my life from that point on! I thank God once again for the wonderful people he placed in my life. The journey would now continue under the guidance, protection, and authority of the church.

Meditation and Reflection

It has taken many years, but I now recognize that this first prophecy was a personal prophecy for me and the ministries that God was calling me to follow. It has been forty years since I had this dream, and by merely closing my eyes, I can recall every visual detail and every word as it has been written on my heart.

I was struck by the fact that in the dream, we as a chosen people were being led into the desert, not unlike the Israelites who were following Moses. The covenant that Christ is offering us today is the same covenant he gave to the Israelites. He wants to lead us out of the bondage of our suffering and into his promised land, which is the kingdom of God.

Are we any different than these ancestors, who saw the hand of God deliver them from slavery and their bondage to the Egyptians? They grew more and more complacent as they followed Moses to the promised land; they complained about their hunger and thirst in spite of God sending them first manna and then quail to feed them. Failing to acknowledge God's actions in their lives, they built idols and turned from trusting God to relying on their own wills to carry them through life. For forty years, an entire generation was left to wander in the desert. For many, their faith and trust in God were lost. Again and again, God continued to call forth his chosen people and announce his presence to them. He is a God who follows us through history, and he is calling us to himself once again.

Many in this generation are the same as these Old Testament Israelites who forgot their God. How many of us abandoned the faith of our ancestors who struggled to come to this country as immigrants with nothing but the clothes on their backs? They came to escape oppression, poverty, and wars. They came to seek freedom in a new land, relying on their faith in God.

Today, the makeup of our families has changed. Lives are noisy with activities, computers, iPhones, careers, sports, and endless programmed activities for our children. Many families are faced with poverty and are disenfranchised by society, which is unwilling or unable to answer their needs. Excuses are made against organized religion, and the mention of God is being removed from our society since it is no longer politically correct. As a result, a generation of children is being lost and the violence of man's inhumanity to man is growing exponentially.

Many of our children are no longer formed in conscience by their parents, by the community in the absence of their parents, or by the reinforcement of religious guidance. Left to their own devices, they find their sense of right and wrong from the media, from gangs, and from anyone who has designs to manipulate them. They turn to their idols, rock stars, movie stars, and sports figures that they place on pedestals, only to see them fall from grace again and again. These same idols would appear to have everything we are programmed to want: fame, talent, wealth, power, and beauty. Yet these same idols are often the victims of their own destruction. They have not found anything bigger than themselves, and, in their restlessness, they want for something that they cannot even name. They long for the peace and freedom to be able to tear away the masks they wear for their followers and to be loved for who they are at the core of their being. It is the same unconditional love that we all desire and that can only be fulfilled by God.

We all hunger and thirst for something more in life and yet are unable to define our needs. Our hearts will remain restless until they find their peace in God.

God is reaching out to us and calling us to find our way back to him. He wants to lead us away from the evil and destruction of this age into the light of his Holy Spirit. Living our lives in and through Christ, we will find ourselves in his kingdom on earth, where we will find happiness, healing, and a peace beyond measure.

Reflection:

- Do I trust God?
- How was I formed in faith?
- What are the idols that keep me from God?
- Do I believe that God abides in me?

Tree of Life (Revelation 22:2)

The little child
Watch the little child
as she reaches for the leaf
far above her

At first
she does not want to jump
but in order to carry it home
She must jump

She anticipates
and wonders
Will she fall again?
Is it worth the risk?

Her eyes
Meet with her companion
The faithful one who has
Been with her
Through time and space
And shared humanity

With a strength not her own
She leaps
And touches the leaf
She falls but not in death
Instead to healing and fullness of life.

CHAPTER 2

Community and Inner Healing

At my pastor's direction, I sought out Father Carl Recker for spiritual guidance. One of the first things that Father Carl told me to do was to find a community where I could learn to grow and use the gifts that God bestowed on me. He suggested that a good place to start was the Charismatic Prayer Group in my parish, which was a mature and thriving community. Before I attended my first meeting, I meditated on what church and community meant for me. I was not one who enjoyed being in groups or to giving up my anonymity. This was not going to be easy!

I was brought up as a Roman Catholic and a Byzantine Catholic. What I knew about God was formed by my village. I grew up for the first seven years of my life in a peninsula of land surrounded by oil refineries and chemical plants on three sides. Tremley Point in Linden, New Jersey, was an oasis of houses, whose yards were outlined with hedges that encased rose gardens with Blessed Virgin Mary statues in bathtubs, along with vegetable gardens that smelled of tomatoes and parsley. Most of our neighbors were of Eastern European ethnicity, and the older generations spoke little English.

My family lived in a three-family house owned by my grandmother, who was the matriarch of our family. My cousin Joanne and I were the same age. She lived with my aunt and uncle on the first floor, my grandparents and uncle on the second floor, and my family on the third floor. Baba, our grandmother, was Joanne's and my caregiver when our parents worked. We were taught right from wrong and had a very good sense of hell. When you grow up with the plumes of fire from the refineries, lighting the sky around your house, the fires of hell take on real visual significance. Living on the third floor, I had the greatest advantage of this hellish reminder since the night sky was always ablaze.

Baba's favorite form of punishment was to lay on the guilt. She would make my cousin and I pray before the statues of the Virgin Mary and the Sacred Heart of Jesus to ask forgiveness for whatever mischief we had perpetrated. She would light the candles, and Joanne and I would kneel in remorse for our penance. Uncle Tommy, who was our senior by ten years, would shuffle his feet across the wool carpet and hit the metal switch plate to send sparks flying with the announcement, "You two better watch out, or the Holy Ghost will get you." Needless to say, Joanne and I would seek holiness wherever we could find it.

In the onion-domed Byzantine church named after St. George, Joanne and I would attend daily Mass with Baba. We meditated on the frescos on the ceiling, the image of St. George slaying the dragon with bloody splashes on the side altar, and we pondered what the red velvet drape behind the main altar was covering up. We had heard that when the new pastor came to the parish, he decided that the mural was too bloody for the parishioners to see every Sunday, so he commissioned a drape to be made by the Altar Society. Joanne and my imaginings were probably far worse than the actual mural. When given the evil eye by my grandmother, we learned to sing the Mass in Slovak while voting on the ugliest babushkas. Joanne and I were a very intelligent team and could conjure up great mischief.

Back in those days, children could wander at will throughout the neighborhood that was comprised of six square blocks, and no one feared for our safety. As children, we knew that if we were good and brought souls to God, we would find our reward in heaven. Thus began our entrepreneurial venture of selling tours to the church of the Holy Family to all of our non-Catholic friends. The proceeds from our evangelization efforts went into the poor box or were used to light a candle for the Blessed Mother. God protected us and the church the day we dropped the lighted match on the floor during one of our tours. Uncle Joe recognized the line of tricycles outside of the church and came to our rescue before any harm was done. However, we were barred from any further evangelization efforts.

This episode was followed closely by the explosion of several tanks in the refinery. The sky was blackened for days, and the winds of the firestorm buffeted our windows. It seemed as if the whole of the landscape was caught up in flames. Our entire family and some of our closest neighbors gathered in prayer in the darkened house, illuminated only by the fire outside and the candles burning in front of the statues of Jesus and Mary. A shrine was set up in the center of the house, and a continuous rosary was prayed for the safety of the neighborhood and the firefighters. My beloved uncle Joe, who was fighting this blaze for five days as a firefighter, was returned to us exhausted but safe from harm. From this experience, I learned the power of prayer to calm my fears and intercede for good.

This was my village, the family and neighbors who gathered to bake for baptisms, weddings, funerals, and who made tens of thousands of perogies to help finance the church. They gathered in prayer for special intentions and entered our house with the greeting in Slovak, "Christ is Risen." Our response was, "Indeed, he has risen." I grew up surrounded by the love of my community. When they stood and celebrated my baptism, they gave more than their word to helping me grow in faith. This community led me by example to understand the meaning of the church. Formation by this community of love is the basis of my faith. The wrenching from this community was the source of my brokenness. Apart from them, I entered my silence.

My family moved in with my other grandmother while our house was being built nearby. My paternal grandmother Perrine had suffered great loss in her life and found comfort in prayer. She was a contemplative who was gentle and kind. She taught me about the beauty in nature and the healing power in prayer. Because of her quiet nature, prior to moving in with her, my mother told me that I would not be allowed to have friends in the house; therefore, I never made friends at school, and I became more and more solitary. Books became my only friends, and silence my companion. Every day, my grandmother and I waited on the front porch for the Black maid who worked for a demanding woman just down the street. My grandmother would wave, walk with her to the bus, and sometimes give her flowers, fresh vegetables, homemade jellies, or bunches of herbs. We never talked about prejudice. I learned by example to love everyone regardless of their color or creed.

When we finally moved into our new home, once again, I was forced into solitude. My parents both worked full time. There was no term back then that would have labeled me a "latchkey child," but that is exactly what I was. Rather than come home to an empty house, as a seven-year-old, I had to take two buses to travel ten miles to my grandmother's house. If I missed the first bus, I would have to wait in the dusk or dark for a second bus, one town over. I obsessed with fear all day long at school, hoping I would not miss the first bus. It became a huge distraction to me and caused me to withdraw more and more into myself. This fear was written on my face.

One day, as I waited for the bus after school with all of my classmates and their mothers who were going to a play at a local venue, I overheard one of the mothers say, "That Judy is one spooky kid. I don't want her coming to my daughter's party." The other mothers agreed, and now, I was convinced that there was something wrong with me that kept me from having friends. This, combined with the debasing from my own mother—who repeatedly told me she was "sorry I was ever born," to "get out of her sight," to "do something about the way that I looked," and "Why can't you do anything right?"—all disparaging remarks that led to the insecurities and fear of intimate relationships that I not only grew up with, but also carried into my adulthood. Let this be a reminder to all of us to always speak with kindness around our children as words alone will make or break a child. When repeated over and over again, they will leave a wound that can only be saved by unconditional love.

As I was experiencing healing, God showed me all of these times when he heard me in my sorrow and nurtured me. He said, *"Do you remember your dream of seeing my mother come rescue you on the playground? I sent you my Blessed Mother as a gift. Do you remember learning to pray the rosary that year? It became your source of courage and strength. You prayed the rosary on the bus trips you feared and all through your life. It has been your strength. Do you remember the bus driver who looked for you every day and even waited for you the day you thought you would be late and miss the bus? I have always placed people in your life to watch over you. I never left you alone! When you thought that no one came to your programs at school, my Mother and I sat in the first row."*

My life did not become any easier as I moved into my teen years. I had the after-school responsibility of taking care of my sister, cooking, cleaning, washing, and ironing, leaving no time for friendships. Everything I did had to meet the mark of perfection! Feeling as though I were a failure and tired of trying to meet what I felt were unattainable expectations, I thought of how I could end my life. I realized that this would be a terrible sin, so I decided to offer God a novena of nine first Fridays. This was no easy venture as I had to leave home an hour and a half early for school and find a church near my high school that I could attend.

In the greatest of God's revelations, he showed me what he did for me in those nine months. He told me that the intercessions of my grandmothers were constant, and I was reminded how, during this time, they always left me saying, "I am praying for you. Don't give up" or "My beautiful, beautiful daughter, be strong." God also gave me the friendship of a wonderful chemistry teacher, who had survived Auschwitz and who had a profoundly spiritual nature. He would often say that one day, I would become a beautiful chemist. Before this time, no one besides my grandmothers had ever called me beautiful or given me the affirmation that I was smart enough to amount to anything. The Lord then showed me that he sent my future husband to me at the end of the nine months. This was an incredible gift. My wonderful husband Jim has remained at my side for fifty-five years and taught me about love, life, humor, and faith.

In all of the healing that I experienced, I came to know a God whose love is unconditional and who never leaves our side. He hears every prayer we ever pray and the prayers that others pray for us, and he answers them. What we pray for may not be what God intends for us for he knows what we need the most. Our prayer should be one of trust in God, who knows all things, can do all things, and is greater than all our imaginings.

I now had to trust that the Charismatic community that I was seeking out was the next step on my journey. But really, a Charismatic Prayer Group? Weren't they supposed to be a little crazy? I had no idea what I was going to find when I attended my first meeting.

What I found was an open and welcoming group of twenty people, who introduced themselves with a warm and embracing welcome. I was surprised to find so many parishioners there who I knew but did not know to be Charismatic. One of my first thoughts was that these were solid individuals who I regarded as good Catholics. The music and worship that followed was beautiful, but the greatest surprise of all was to find them singing in tongues. To me, it was like the sound of angels, and since I already had the gift, I could easily join in. I knew that finally, I had found a safe haven and a loving community. They gave language to my experiences, and I was to learn through them the depth and scope of my charism of prophecy and healing.

Reflection:

The Lord tells us in the gospel of Luke (Luke 12:4–7) that not a sparrow is neglected by him. He has counted every hair on our heads and goes on to say:

> *Do not worry about your life and what you will eat, or about your body and what you will wear. For life is more than food and body more than clothing. Notice the ravens: they do not sow or reap; they have neither storehouse nor barn, yet God feeds them. How much more important are you than birds! Can any of you by worrying add a moment to your lifespan? If even the smallest things are beyond your control, why be anxious about the rest? Notice how the flowers grow. They do not toil or spin. But I tell you not even Solomon in all his splendor was dressed like one of them. If God so clothes the grass in the field that grows today and is thrown into the oven tomorrow, will he not provide for you of little faith? As for you, do not seek what you are to eat and what you are to drink, do not worry anymore. All the nations of the world seek for these things, and your father knows that you need them. Instead, seek His kingdom and these other things will be given to you besides. (Luke 12:22–31)*

So many of our lives today are broken and have an unspoken need. We live an inner life of wanting and searching for unconditional love. Sometimes, the very affirmations we seek are simply unattainable because the person from whom we seek them are themselves hurting and broken too. It is easy to live in a spiral of brokenness that is passed on from one generation to the next!

Who, but God, sees us as we were created to be? He knows our wants and our needs often before we are aware of them ourselves. He desires us to be whole and at peace with who we are and who we were created to be. Our uniqueness is a reason to celebrate for each of us is created in the image and likeness of God. When we are able to surrender to all that is beautiful and complete within us, we are free to serve those around us in the light of our transformation.

This transformation is not without pain. We need to rid ourselves of the familiar and comfortable mechanisms that help us cope. We must surrender to God completely all of our hurts, bad habits, unforgiveness, and all of our transgressions that have kept us from being whole. Just as the refiner's fire draws out the impurities that weaken the gold, so, too, must we be purged of the sins that have marred both our lives and our souls. We need to forgive all who have injured us and seek forgiveness from those we may have hurt in our brokenness. This is a process that cannot be accomplished without the unconditional love that comes from God. When we see ourselves in our own brokenness and sin, it is punishing and totally masochistic. Without God's love to redeem us, we cannot take on this task.

Looking at our own darkness can leave us in a void so abject that we cannot function. One realizes that we are left to fall into an abyss that would separate us from all those around us and from God. Only by the umbilical of God's love can we live! This is the redeeming love of Christ, who offered himself up to death on a cross to take on the sins of the world. This is the love that makes us complete!

Through the power of the love of the Father for his son Jesus and Jesus's all-consuming love for the Father is a love so complete that itself is the third person of the Most Holy Trinity, the Holy Spirit. This is the spirit of God that abides in us. I like to think of the Holy Spirit as the umbilical that connects all of our earthly beings into a relationship with both the Father and the Son. We can only be separated from God by willfully choosing a path of sin and evil. Our existence in and the development of our earthly being is tethered to God by this umbilical of love that empowers us and nourishes us in this life. All that we are and all who we were created to be is present within us from the moment that we are created and named by God. However, God gave us free will, and it is up to us to choose who we will become. Do we seek God's will, choose to struggle through life by our own will, or do we choose the path of sin?

The path to becoming whole, holy, and complete only requires the desire and trust to find God within.

Reflection:

- How does it make you feel to know that God knows every hair on your head and that your name is carved in the palm of his hand?
- Do you pray with an open heart that trusts in God's power to answer your prayer?
- Can you think back to a time when God placed a certain person or people in your life when you most needed them?
- Do you pray in intercession for others, believing that God can bring about miracles?
- Are you willing to trust God to transform your life? Are you willing to surrender the whole of your being to become who God created you to be?

CHAPTER 3

Healing

Then he summoned His twelve disciples and gave them authority over unclean spirits to drive them out and to cure every disease and every illness.

—Matthew 10:1

Throughout Scripture, there are over 375 references to the healing power of God. We know that Jesus drew throngs of people to himself, both by his Word and through the many healings that they witnessed. Jesus then commissioned his disciples to go and heal in his name. Following the Pentecost:

> *Many signs and wonders were done among the people at the hands of the Apostles. (Acts 5:12–16)*

Paul tells us:

> *There are different kinds of spiritual gifts but the same spirit; there are different forms of service but the same Lord; there are different workings but the same God who produces all of them in everyone. To each individual the manifestation of the Spirit is given for*

some benefit. To one is given through the Spirit the expression of wisdom, to another the expression of knowledge according to the same Spirit; to another faith by the same Spirit; to another gifts of healing by the one Spirit; to another mighty deeds; to another prophecy; to another discernment of spirits; to another varieties of tongues; to another interpretation of tongues. But one and the same Spirit produces all of these distributing them individually to each person as he wishes. (1 Corinthians 12:4–11)

Reflecting on my own inner healing, I was in awe of God's presence and love for me that would bring me peace and joy unlike any that I had ever felt before. My entire psyche was opened to a new freedom to let go of the past hurts and to begin life anew. I began to see how I operated out of the brokenness I had carried with me from my childhood—the insecurities, the fear of abandonment, and the fear of letting people get close to me lest they see my inadequacies. The Lord had brought me out of the darkness into the light. As my inner child was healed, I could see how I had developed a shield to keep people from getting close to me; I had become reluctant to develop close friendships. I was obsessive and compulsive in my need to be perfect, and I rejected failure at all costs. As a result, I had a tendency to be controlling without being confrontational—truly a passive-aggressive personality.

Through my own healing, I was drawn to scripture and the many ways that Jesus and his disciples healed throughout their ministries. I particularly found that both Paul's and Luke's witness accounts of healing in Acts of the Apostles spoke to me in new ways. I began to read books by modern-day priests who had the gifts of healing. I grew in wonder and awe of how God was acting in my church, and I felt a deep sense of knowing that God had plans for me in this ministry. However, I had no idea how this gift would manifest.

One night, I received a call from my sister, who poured out her heart to me and asked if I could come be with her. Her husband had fallen into a deep depression. I told her that I needed two days to make arrangements for the care of my sons before I could fly out to be with her.

Meanwhile, I told her to pray and trust God to provide us with answers on how to proceed with his care. That night, I was awakened at 3:00 a.m. by the Holy Spirit. I placed myself in silent prayer and listened to our Lord. He showed me his love for this man and gave me the words to say to him that would release him from his inner turmoil. This shook me to the very core of my being, and I was truly reluctant to confront anyone with this knowledge lest I be in error that it was truly the Lord who had revealed this to me. However, I could not ignore such a commanding voice that said, *"I tell you to wake him in the night and tell him to go and watch the sun rise. Tell him that this is the beginning of a new day and a new life. Tell him to go to Sunday Mass today and meet me in the Eucharist."*

I was shaken and was filled with an indescribable energy that passed through my body, like none that I had experienced before. I knew that I had to obey and follow through on what I was being asked to do. I called my sister and told her to put her husband on the phone at 4:30 a.m., and I relayed to him what the Lord had spoken to me. At noon of that same day, I received a call from him saying that he had been healed—for truly only God would know what had caused his pain. When he went to noon Mass, the opening hymn was "He lifts us up on eagle's wings and bears us on the breath of *dawn* and makes us shine like the sun; and holds us in the palms of his hands."

His psychiatrist called me several days later and asked how this happened. He said it would have taken years of therapy to bring this man this kind of healing. It turned out that this doctor was in prayer about leaving his practice at this major university hospital to start a Christian practice. This healing was his discernment.

Following this experience, I immediately went to my spiritual director to let him know what happened. He sent me home with a load of books on healing in the church, particularly those by the Linn brothers[1] on inner healing. It was shortly after that when I attended my first Charismatic Mass. During that Mass, my hands were burning with an energy that flowed out from them. It was after Communion that Father Recker called on the congregation to reach out to the people around us and lay hands on them, saying that the Lord intended to heal us through the Eucharist. I knew then beyond any doubt that I had received the gift of healing. That was the beginning of a ministry of healing that opened my eyes to all that God intended for his people. Many other experiences have shown me the real presence of Jesus in the Eucharist and his desire to heal us and make us whole.

One instance in particular, I was at a regular Sunday Mass, and during the homily, I heard the Lord say, *"I want you to turn to the man behind you and tell him to go to the Eucharist, expecting to be healed."* I began to argue with the Lord that this was not a Charismatic Mass. I would be out of order to act, and how did I really know it was God and not myself, or worse yet the evil one? The Lord said, *"He is very bald."* Not seeing the man come in, I had no idea who was sitting behind me. When the place in the Mass for the sign of peace occurred, my temples were throbbing (a manifestation of the gifts of prophecy or healing for me), and I felt as though someone had taken me by the shoulders and spun me around. I passed this message on to the very bald man sitting directly behind me. I told him that the Lord wanted him to "approach the Eucharist expecting to be healed," and I asked him if that made any sense to him.

---

[1]   Dennis Linn, SJ, and Matthew Linn, SJ, *Healing of Memories* (New York/ Mahwah, NJ: Paulist Press, 1974).

He responded, "No."

He left the pew and his wife said, "Maybe it makes no sense to him, but it means everything to me!" Shortly thereafter, he returned from receiving the Eucharist with tears flowing down his face.

I said to the Lord, "What was that about?"

He responded, *"Oh, that my people would come to the Eucharist every Sunday expecting to be healed."*

I turned myself into the pastor the next day, telling him what I had done and should someone come to him about the incident, it was me who was to blame. Several weeks later, the pastor told me that in fact, the gentleman came to him and said, "Some lady with vibes told me to go to the Eucharist expecting to be healed." He wanted to let the priest know that he had indeed been healed.

How often do we go to Mass thinking we are checking the box? Many go to church because we were trained by our parents to do so. It is our inherited faith. So many of us have never *owned* our faith! It is not unusual to have fallen away from organized religion when, as young adults, we were on our own. I have known many people who, during their years of searching, seek out other faiths or philosophies until they reach a spiritual awareness around the age of thirty-five or when they have children of their own. It is then that they begin their search for what they themselves believe. It is a spiritual maturing. Still, many attend church and complain that the church doesn't answer their need, the homilies are boring, the music is bad, they don't have enough time in their week, and they find infinite reasons to angst. Yet Jesus says, *"Come, find me, know that I am your bread of life, your manna. I am the Word, hear me. Come to the Eucharist and embrace me. Come expectant knowing I am truly here."*

I am forever humbled by what Jesus does for us. We can never take credit for having anything to do with the healings that we witness. We are merely empty vessels who God uses when and how he chooses. I am often left with tears at the miracles that God brings about through his Holy Spirit, and I am always surprised at his goodness and incredible mercy, even in the most dysfunctional situations. We need to reflect on the true presence of Christ in the Eucharist. No one needs to lay hands on you to pray if you believe in Jesus's true presence in the Eucharist. As we open our hands to receive Jesus as the true bread of life, we are greater than the woman who reached out to touch the hem of his garment to be healed of her hemorrhage (Luke 8:43–48). At that moment of encounter, we hold in the palm of our hands the whole embrace of Christ.

It might be discouraging at times when you pray for a person over many months or years and you do not see the miracles you hoped to see. You quickly learn that it is not a matter of faith or the person's worthiness that is the obstacle since we are all loved equally by God. Rather, it is how God wants to heal us for the greatest healing of all is spiritual healing, then emotional healing, and lastly, physical healing. Jesus reminds us to be persistent in our prayer and that his time is not always our time.

When healing is gradual, one has time to process and reflect on the change. But when a person is miraculously healed, it can be alarming! How does one process this instantaneous change to their life? The euphoria can be intoxicating. People around them are not sure how to relate to them. Anyone outside of a religious realm thinks they are crazy.

Over the many years in the healing ministry, I have been able to witness unbelievable miracles. We have an awesome God who is as present to us today as when he walked the earth. I have heard the witness of doctors who were astounded at the healings they never believed would be possible. Yet with God, all things are possible.

One of my summer jobs was as an intern chemist at an electroplating company. Once a week, I was required to work in a clean room that had no windows. For eight hours, I would carry out a tedious process of analysis for quality control of computer connectors. I hated the tedium and the isolation required, yet there was a woman who did this every day for eight hours and had done so for many years. I asked her how she did it. Her response was that she had bad karma in this life and had to accept that she would never be happy. She believed that her next life would be better if she suffered through this life. I was young, and I was left speechless. As I look back, I have pondered her response many times. I am happy that I am a Christian, and Jesus, the incarnate, who is my salvation, has paved the way for me to everlasting life in heaven. I did not need to be recycled or to worry about what I might come back as in the next life. Jesus wants us to be whole and holy in this life and to be happy with him forever in heaven.

Do we realize the gift that we have been given by Jesus's death and resurrection? I hesitate to think of how much grain and how many doves and carcasses of animals I would have to present at the temple if Jesus had not conquered my sins by his death on the cross. His resurrection showed us that our lives do not end when our bodies give out, but come to life through Christ. This world is the womb in which we are formed for rebirth into life in heaven. Jesus calls us to be whole and holy in this life and to be happy with him in the everlasting life to come!

Reflection:

- Where are you on your faith journey? Are you still at the stage of inherited faith?
- Are you still searching for what you believe?
- Do you own your faith, coming to believe for yourself?
- Do you believe in the healing power of prayer?

CHAPTER 4

The Fourth Dimension Living in the Kingdom of God

Eye has not seen, and ear has not heard, and what has not entered the human heart, what God has prepared for those who love Him.
—1 Corinthians 2:9

When we think of the kingdom of God, we think of it as the heaven that we aspire to or an Eden yet to be realized here on earth. Yet Jesus tells us that the kingdom of God is at hand. He taught us to pray, "*Your Kingdom come, on earth, as it is in heaven*" (Matthew 6:9–13).

The kingdom of God is truly at hand, yet we do not take the time to seek it or recognize it when it is right in front of us. We call it a coincidence when all things come together in unexpected ways. Albert Einstein said, "Coincidence is God's way of remaining anonymous." Is that true, or does God want us to know that he is present and that the kingdom of God is at hand? We as a church belong to the mystical body of Christ.

When experiencing the presence of God in contemplation, I like to call it the "between place." It is the quiet that is between consciousness and sleeping. There is a peace that comes over you, where you experience a kind of euphoria that is a delight beyond knowing. Your whole being wants to stay there for the bliss is all-encompassing. As you leave this "between place" to return to full consciousness, there is a new awareness, a knowing not previously experienced. You need to reflect on what knowledge has been imparted to you during this encounter, and you need to seek out God's words in Scripture for discernment.

If only we would recognize the incredible gift that this friendship with Christ truly is, it is here that we experience the kingdom among us, along with the peace, love, and possibilities that we have for our existence. We would soon know that we are not alone in this world and that Jesus is truly present to us in every moment. Our prayers are not falling on deaf ears. Our God hears our prayers. He will make good of all that befalls us. Christ, in his suffering, took on our pain. Our prayers are indeed answered, perhaps not in the ways we would initially choose them to be answered, but in the end, the answers bring us to a greater good.

In this "between space," when God first spoke to me, he showed me all of the prayers I had prayed as a child and the ways he answered them. He showed me the people, experiences, and love by which he sustained me. He showed me our Blessed Mother, who was ever at my side, praying for my safety. Over and over, I felt her loving presence and trusted in her prayers for me. Mary is the Ark of the Covenant, who carried our precious Jesus in her body, and she will strike at the head of Satan and destroy him. She, too, is present in our kingdom here on earth as her advocacy to our King of kings carries great weight. It is Mary's intercessions that lead us to the indwelling of the Trinity—the Father, Son, and Holy Spirit.

The Trinity is the triumphant God who has given us this kingdom on earth. Those who recognize this gift are connected in a way beyond knowing. I will later give voice to a few of the great miracles that have occurred through the belief that his kingdom is at hand. It is our reason for hope in an age of great offenses of evil creeping into our world. We have a battle at hand, and we can only find peace and happiness if we begin to join with others to bring God's intentions into our lives and into the lives of others. One by one, two by two, we will come to a place of safety, love, true peace, and happiness as we are joined in relationship to one another.

Over and over, I have experienced the overwhelming love that God has for us and how we are all connected through his indwelling. One day, while driving, I was praying when my dear friend Allison came to mind. She taught high school girls who were incarcerated. I was so overcome with a need to pray for her profusely, which I did. Later that day, I called her and asked her what happened that caused me to have to pray for her so intensely. She told me that one of the girls had attacked her viciously. She said that at that moment, she experienced the presence of Christ in the room and began to pray as well. She was rescued by an administrator. Afterward, the nurse who treated her was amazed that she was not more seriously injured.

On another occasion, I was cleaning my house and vacuuming when, as I was praying, a coworker came to mind, and I began weeping uncontrollably for no reason. I later called her and asked about her day. She told me that she was in court seeking custody of her children from her abusive husband, who appeared to be a model of the community. The previous time she was in court, they had to call a recess since she could not stop crying. This was the rescheduled court date, and she prayed that she would not cry until she gave her testimony. She said she did not shed a tear and was able to get through all the court proceedings. I told her what had happened, and I knew that God had answered her prayers and given me her tears. In the end, she was granted custody. I did not know her story before this event.

I now trust that when someone or something comes into my mind, I should not ignore it but either pray or act. I will make a phone call at the very moment that a call is needed.

I was blessed when my fourth child was born and had to return to the hospital only hours after we had brought him home. Test results showed that he had extremely high bilirubin levels. Upon our arrival, since he could not be returned to the nursery, he had to be placed in the pediatric unit. Somehow, word got out that our son was in the hospital, and the physician who was on duty was someone I had hired years ago, prior to his getting into medical school. A nurse I knew insisted she be on duty day and night at my son's side. A stream of people who worked in the hospital came by to offer assistance. The nurse on duty asked who I was, since she had never seen such love as she saw that day, with so many willing to help. I told her that this was my church community from several parishes, who came to know me through healing prayer events. We were doubly blessed that the nurse was on duty by Ryan's side that night since his incubator overheated, and she instantly removed him when the alarm went off. This, for me, was further proof that the Holy Spirit connects all who believe.

Our living Christ is ever present to us and desires us to call upon him in prayer. He will reveal himself to us, in the hour of our need. When you are open to his presence and intervention in our lives, you will be overcome in wonder and awe at the connection of all things working for the good. You will know that God is real.

I sat on the diocesan board of the Charismatic Renewal and served on the Word Gifts Committee. People on this committee have discerned gifts of prophecy, discernment, wisdom, and knowledge. As the board, we were developing the theme for the next annual conference. All of us on Word Gifts were asked to go home and pray for the Lord to reveal the theme for this big event. We left to return to our homes that spanned several counties and returned two weeks later. We all came back with the same word that the Holy Spirit imparted to us: "Jesus as the Fountain of Life." We had received prophetic words, visions, and biblical passages that discerned this theme. Time, distance, and lack of verbal communication between us did not matter for what God had intended to speak to his people. Jesus is the fountain of life. "We who know him will never thirst.

We are washed clean by his passion, and we are brought to new life through our baptism." We truly are one body in Christ, connected by his Spirit.

Our prayer and openness to God's presence in our lives brings about every possibility, even beyond our imaginings. One day, in prayer, I heard the Lord say that he was gifting me with a ring of twelve gems (Revelations 21:18–20, Exodus 28:15–21). I was the diamond since *"I was strong in faith and unwavering in purpose to serve the kingdom of God."* At this time, I had no awareness that "gems" coming together had the biblical significance of being a sign of divine creation.

Several days later, a new neighbor came to visit me and asked if I believed in the prophetic gifts in the church. I told her that I did. She then said that the Lord told her that *"she was the emerald and God was the gem cutter."* Did this make sense to me? I was totally amazed, never questioning that this was God's doing. The next week, two women from my parish approached me and said we were supposed to pray together. One revealed that God called her the onyx, and the other he called the sapphire. The four of us came together to pray in silence and seek God's guidance. I went to my spiritual director and shared with him what I was experiencing, and he encouraged me to keep him up to date on how this was progressing.

Several weeks later, the Lord encouraged me to reach out to a woman in another parish, who I met on a recent retreat, and ask her if she had a sense of God calling her to pray with a group of women. She responded, "Yes." I also asked if she had a sense of anyone else who might be called and she said, "Yes, she is standing right here with me." I invited both ladies to join us for prayer. I learned later that the Lord called one a diamond and the other a ruby. Next, I met a young woman on a retreat in Michigan, and the Lord said, *"Behold, the one with whom you will pray."* We counted off from one to fourteen to form prayer groups for the weekend. She and I were both numbered as "one." That was the beginning of over forty years of praying together. Her incredible gifts of teaching, healing, and music still fill my heart. Her gem is a chalcedony.

Soon after in prayer, I heard the Lord say that the next person would come to me with the message of salvation, and she would be a topaz. A month later, a young woman called me from another county and asked if we could meet. She said that she had heard me give a talk on salvation at a "Life in the Spirit" retreat and that she had been asked to do the same at the next monthly retreat sponsored by the diocese. She wanted some help with the talk. When I asked her if the gem topaz had any meaning to her, she told me that her husband was marketing a car called the Topaz. When the twelve gems were in place, I told Father Carl, who said that we were to form a healing ministry. We had the blessings of the bishop to form others in healing and to give healing retreats. Father Carl was to be our spiritual director on these retreats, and he told us that we should be ready to begin the first retreat in two months. The bishop also indicated that he would vouch for us if we were ever questioned about our ministry.

Our group met every Saturday morning for Mass and contemplative prayer at Lourdes College, Franciscan House of Prayer, to listen for God's word of guidance and formation. We as a group were given the ministry of forming others throughout the diocese in healing prayer.

Truly, we were strangers to each other, whom God formed in spiritual friendship. We broke bread and shared life with a newfound intimacy. The Lord enhanced our gifts to bring healing and life to so many of his people. We witnessed many, many miracles beyond our imaginings as God healed his people, even to the astonishment of the medical community.

The Lord promised the "gems" that he "*would scatter us from north to south and east to west.*" It is now forty years later, and those of us still alive have indeed been scattered throughout the country. We continue to pray healing prayer and evangelize. Of the twelve gems, one remains in pastoral ministry, another has authored several books, has evangelized across the country, and has served on the National Committee for the Charismatic Renewal. Another was our historian and technical guru. She has started and supported many ministries with her gifts. While another has published and recorded her sacred music for healing and worship, she taught theology at a university, and she has evangelized across the country. Another brings music, wisdom, and healing throughout the diocese of Toledo, Ohio. The remaining gems moved around the country and served in a variety of church ministries, and some have sadly passed on. One was a living example of unconditional love, and another showed us all how to die with dignity.

Our eyes need to be opened to the kingdom of God that is within our grasp. Our Lord is calling us to gather as our society crumbles into outrage, sacrilege, and denial of a God greater than themselves. A pervasive evil is beginning to influence those who are susceptible. Our God wants to bring us a hope beyond measure that is born of love and which connects us all. We are indeed the mystical body of Christ, together with his angels and his saints. We were formed in love to be love.

The spiritual life is our fourth dimension. It exists in and through Christ, present in the Trinity. The church as the mystical body of Christ intends to gather us all into her realm, the kingdom of God on earth.

> *I heard a voice from the throne saying, "Behold, God's dwelling is with the human race. He will dwell with them and they will be his people and God himself will be with them. He will wipe every tear from their eyes, and there will be no more death or mourning, wailing or pain, the old order has passed away."*
> *(Revelations 21:3–4)*

Prophecy of Hope

Man can control people, history, and events, but no one can keep my people from me. See how easy it is for me to slip in the night and conquer evil with good and gather my people to me.

Reflection:

- Recall a time when you felt that God was calling you to reach out to someone in need.
- Reflect on an event in your life where you experienced actions coming together in unexpected ways.
- Do you believe that the Holy Spirit may be awakening gifts in you? If so, how is he asking you to use them?
- Journal a time in your life where you may have experienced a glimpse of this fourth dimension.

CHAPTER 5

Discernment, Deliverance, and the Power of the Priesthood

Recalling when God first presented his gifts to me, he said that the greatest of my gifts was that of discernment. At the time, I did not fully understand how this gift would influence my life. Remembering this first encounter of being faced by evil in the presence of the mind reader that I mentioned previously, I should have been prepared for other occasions. It was certainly not an experience that I would desire to encounter again, nor a gift that I would encourage others to delve into. Evil is real and entertained too easily in our culture.

While leading a group of high school students in a small group within the church, I found out that many of the teenage girls were experimenting with Ouija boards, tarot cards, and seances in party settings. My spirit quaked to hear this, and I cautioned them about the dangers and destruction to which these activities could lead. The occult is real, and evil looks for an opening for deceptions. One may be unsuspecting of the true dangers of this activity when seeking out a fortune teller in earnest or for fun. You may hear an element of truth in a first encounter in these settings, which will ultimately lead you to a lie on a second or be a hook into the occult going forward. An individual can be led into false hope or an unending fear. If we do not stay centered on God in entering the world of the unconscious, we may be caught in the realm of the collective unconscious and the state of the occult.

Truly, these girls experienced great fear and disruption to their relationships as a result of these supposed games. I directed them to seek out a priest and be reconciled with God. As teenagers, there is a natural curiosity to find answers to their lives and hope for their futures; they are easily suspectable to these kinds of activities if they have never been cautioned of their dangers.

One morning, I was about to get my breakfast when I heard the Lord say that he wanted me to fast and pray for the day since he was sending me a person for healing, who could not be prayed with except in the presence of a priest. Before I put a morsel in my mouth, I prayed to the Lord for discernment. I was led to Acts 19:13–16, where the sons of Sceva were confronted by the evil spirit who said, "*Jesus I recognize, and Paul I know, but who are you?*" Needless to say, I was admonished and now very cautious; I fasted and prayed for the remainder of the day. That evening, as the prayer group was near the end of the meeting, there was an opportunity for healing prayer. After several people came forth, the last person in line was accompanied by two other people. The Lord said, "*This is the one with whom you should not pray.*"

As this young woman sat down for prayer, I said that the hour was late, and we could not enter into any lengthy prayer, therefore, we would have to be brief. I suggested that she call me at my home the next day and I would arrange a time for us to meet. I then proceeded to pray the Lord's Prayer over her, and I prayed in tongues briefly since that was the Holy Spirit praying through me. The tongues were decidedly different from any that I had ever prayed as they were harsh and demanding. I ended the prayer quickly. It was past 11:00 p.m. that same night when she called me to set up an appointment and revealed to me that she was not forthcoming in her need for healing prayer. She said she was a princess for Satan in a local cult and was very scared. At that time, there was satanic cult activity being investigated in the community. Whether she was part of that cult or another, I never knew.

The only certainty that I had at that time was that the priests' Holy Orders held a power over evil that none of my gifts could touch. I went to Father Carl and asked how we should proceed; he sent me to Father George Koerber, who had experience with deliverance. When I went to Father George, he asked me what was the matter with Father Carl. It was then that I told them to talk among themselves and get back to me. After conferring with the bishop, it was determined that this individual would be prayed with under the seal of the Sacrament of Reconciliation, with the intercession of the Order of Carmelite Nuns, who agreed to be praying before the Blessed Sacrament during this prayer time. Ultimately, this young woman found the joy of release from this evil. Years later, I met her at a Pentecost Mass. She was leading a procession into church, carrying a banner for her parish. I did not recognize her when she came up to me to introduce herself. She was totally changed in appearance and had witnessed how much Jesus had transformed her life.

I wish that this had been my only encounter with evil, but others came forth, who had been involved with satanic cults. Each had elements of horror leading up to their asking for prayer. I soon became aware that witchcraft was also prevalent in our local society. I would add that there is no such thing as a good witch or a white witch; both are destructive. An FBI agent once asked me to pray for him since he was praying the rosary every morning to strengthen him for the true evil he had encountered in his job. I remember asking Father Carl what was happening. It was as if I had a shingle posted on my door. His response was, "When one has the gift, God leads them to you."

Perhaps the funniest encounter was with a woman who claimed she had visions of the Blessed Mother and had stigmata. Many people from our diocese were traveling a long distance to seek her out for healing. Father Carl asked our healing team to look in on her and discern her supposed gifts. God was good for as our team stopped for lunch, we were seated at a large window in the restaurant; across the street was a shop with a window display for a fortune teller. It had a Blessed Mother statue in the window, along with every kind of occult symbol.

Later, as we gathered with others who were seeking healing in the woman's house, she presented herself in a blue house coat, blue mittens on her hands, fuzzy slippers, and a blue kerchief on her head. She singled out our group after her witness and prayer service and asked us to remain behind. She wanted to know who we were and where we came from. She gave us each a rosary and told us that the Blessed Mother's presence was often accompanied by the scent of roses. On the car ride home in freezing temperatures, we had to open all the car windows so as not to become sickened by the intense smell of the rose oil that had been rubbed on our rosaries. Truly, our God has a wonderful sense of humor. We reported our discernment back to the diocese. Later, we learned that this woman could no longer accept visitors in her home. We continued to pray for her since we did not think she was a charlatan but rather a sick woman who was misguided. There is a hunger in people to seek out signs from God to confirm their beliefs. They will gather to find holy images on grain silos or on the peeling paint on buildings. The true signs that Jesus left us are in the seven sacraments of the church, which are outward signs of his grace. Let Jesus be most present to us through these sacraments.

I thought I could leave this ministry behind when I moved out of state. However, I became a youth minister, where I encountered many troubled teenagers. One of my youths reached out to me to say that she had been involved in a satanic cult and saw her friend come close to being sacrificed. I remembered reading about a similar incident to her description of the event in our local newspaper. This involvement had lasting consequences for her life. I encouraged her to seek out the Sacrament of Reconciliation with our loving pastor.

I am horrified to see that it was recently announced that a superior court was allowing satanic clubs to meet as an after-school activity under the Freedom of Religion Act. We have reached a point of madness in our society, and we are inviting an extreme danger to take root. Each of these individuals mentioned was at the point of great mental anguish and self-destruction. They were fraught with extreme fear when they came forth for healing. This is an abomination to our God! We must stop this now!

Reflection:

- Reflect on whether you knowingly or unknowingly entertain elements of the occult in your life.
- Are your children experiencing darkness in their computer games or TV viewing?
- Challenge anyone who you believe may be entertaining evil in their lives to the great harm this may cause them.

CHAPTER 6
The Open Door: The Ministry of Grace

The city of Toledo, Ohio, was undergoing a renaissance in 1983. Beautiful modern buildings and recreation areas were being developed while people were dying in the streets. There were several reports of homeless people dying of hypothermia that winter. My conscience was bothered by the idea that a person could freeze to death in what I thought to be a caring community. I could not fathom where to begin to remediate this problem since I had no experience as a social worker. Little did I know that my inactivity was about to change.

One day, a friend asked me to come to St. Louis Catholic Church's soup kitchen to pray with a man for healing. John, like so many of the homeless that I have met over my lifetime, was a loving and caring individual, whose life was altered due to untreated mental illness. John was caring for so many of his homeless companions—finding them shelter from the elements, seeking out shoes, looking after the safety of the young people, and not looking after his own needs. It is a long, beautiful story about how John was healed. After one of our meetings, he asked what I saw when I looked at him. I responded, "I see hopelessness, helplessness, weariness, and pain."

He answered, "If you see this, why can't anyone else?" I told him that all could see it, and then he asked, "If that is true, how can a person call themselves a Christian and not do anything about it?" He was hunched over as he walked away from me, and I knew in that moment that I had encountered the Fallen Christ.

I shared this experience and my prayer with my spiritual director, Father Carl, who told me not to go home from our session without finding the homeless a place to live. He told me to call him when I got home. He encouraged me to step in faith for if this was God's work, then God would bring this shelter into being.

Father told me to find my way home via Cherry Street in downtown Toledo. After leaving his office, I had some words with God that were not all that pleasant. I traveled down Cherry Street and encountered people sleeping in doorways, a man climbing out of a dumpster, and a child and mother picking French fries off the floor of a local McDonald's. I saw an abandoned building that was for sale and made arrangements to meet with a realtor. I brought my friend Sandy and her husband Bill, who had been a professional football player, along with me, dressed to the nines. We looked like serious developers.

The building was in ruins, but it had beautiful architectural bones. It had a historical past of being a theater, a girl's school, etc. Its price was prohibited and so far out of range that in my mind, it was not an option. In prayer, I asked the Lord why he had led me there. His response was, *"All of my children were created to be beautiful and perfect just like this building. However, the events and tragedies in their lives caused them ruin. I desire to restore my broken people to the beauty that I created them to be."*

I was convicted and resigned to the fact that this charge could not be put aside. However, this building was beyond my ability to renovate. I persevered and looked up Father Robert Armstrong, who was pastor of St. Louis's church and a champion for the homeless. I nicknamed him Don Quixote because he had a heart and a vision so full, yet despairing for all that he dreamed should be done for the homeless. He told me that there were many in the diocese who would have liked to open a shelter for the homeless, but that there was no funding, and the bishop felt strongly that this had to be a ministry that was raised up by the laity. He recommended that I contact Sister Ann, who was well-connected with Social Services and an expert in 12-Step Programs. She was a most humble, holy, and intelligent religious, whose love for the homeless was boundless. She said she would be on board to support our efforts in any way she could.

While looking for housing for the ministry, it occurred to me that perhaps the diocese had vacant facilities available. My next stop was at the office of Bishop James Hoffman, who knew me well. I went to his office and explained to him what I had in mind. I asked him if he had any houses bequeathed to the diocese that he wanted to give away. You can imagine my surprise when he immediately responded that he had five and that I could take my pick. I was incredulous! Bishop Hoffman said he would not bring the ministry under the jurisdiction of the diocese, but he would rent us the property for $1. He also agreed to pay the insurance on the property. It would be up to me to acquire the continued financing and structure the ministry. He gave me his blessing to go into the Charismatic prayer groups and to use the healing ministry to find support.

With this promise in hand, I now needed a board of directors and seed money. Word got out, and I was led to the director of the Water Street Rescue Mission. This was a well-run, wonderful, large facility for the homeless, led by an experienced director, who reflected the love of the Lord. He, like so many who looked after the homeless population, saw unending needs and limited resources. He identified for me that the greatest need at the time was to serve the population of homeless, who were too frightened or fragile to seek out a large shelter. Because of this great need, he promised that he would support our ministry. What I needed to learn from him were the nuances of the homeless population and the support systems that would benefit them the most. He encouraged me to give a talk at the Full Gospel Men's Club luncheon about the desire to start up a shelter for the homeless, who fell through the cracks.

The day I was to give the luncheon talk, we were in the midst of a very heavy snowstorm; therefore, few people turned out. The twelve men in attendance told me to save the talk for another time and just chat about what my vision was for this ministry. I told them that my greatest need was to find a board of directors for the ministry. They turned to each other, shrugged their shoulders, and said, "Here we are." On this board-to-be was an accountant, an attorney, a public relations specialist, a specialist in Veteran Affairs, a person who agreed to live on-site as house director, etc. One by one, they committed themselves to the start-up of the Open Door Ministry. A colleague of the director, who agreed to serve on the board, was a member of the Wesleyan Methodist Church, which had an "umbrella organization" for new start-up Christian ministries. They would take over the responsibility for accounting and licensor of the new organization until it could stand alone. This would assure us that the Open Door had oversight and would operate within the framework of the law.

The beauty of the Open Door Ministry is that it was a complete and a perfect coming together of the ecumenical community. The love of God and the power of the Holy Spirit were celebrated in our midst. The deepest respect for God's action superseded our differences.

The diocese of Toledo, at the time, was completing Renew, a program centered on discipleship. Throughout the diocese, small groups of individuals shared faith in neighborhood settings. My neighborhood just happened to have a very blessed population, who felt called to support the start-up of the Open Door Ministry by donating $5,000 in seed money. They also contributed materials and manpower to clean up a house on Cherry Street and furnish it for our first residents. My husband was finishing the rec room in the basement of our house as his "do-it-yourself" project and was often surprised to find his Sheetrock, plumbing supplies, etc. missing.

It took three months from hearing the promptings of the Lord to welcoming our first residents into the Open Door. It was March 1, 1984. The Lord led the young, the old, the sick, and the dying to us. There are amazing stories of miracles, lives reconciled, and lives transformed. The special people who passed through this ministry left knowing that there were people who cared about them and a God who loved them unconditionally. The mission of the Open Door Ministry was a faith-centered ministry that existed to welcome all: to respect the dignity and self-worth of each man, to recognize the spiritual need of each one who has lost hope, and to reach out with love in order to raise each man to his fullest potential, regardless of emotional, mental, physical, or financial handicaps.

The fruits of the Holy Spirit leading and guiding this ministry are evident as the ministry has continued to grow and is an example of God's desire to heal his people. As of this writing, this ministry is approaching its fortieth year of existence. There are now three facilities and hundreds of homeless have been restored to productive lives. The last director of the Open Door[2] served the ministry for thirteen years and, in that time alone, gave witness to the fact that 845 men returned to sober living and productive lives.

God's love and protection for this ministry was always evident. We could see the gospel come alive in our midst. One of my favorite stories was the day the Open Door ran out of toilet paper. I had just bought twenty rolls, so this seemed incredulous to me. My first thought was that illness had hit the house, but I was assured that this was not the case. I told Jeff Comeau, who was the resident director at the time, that I would buy some and bring it as soon as I fed my children. It was an hour later that Jeff called and said, "Don't hurry with the toilet paper. An old woman came by and called from the sidewalk for help. She said she had a donation to give the ministry, but she could not carry anything more than what she had in the shopping bag. She said that she needed someone to carry it up the

---

[2]   Open Door Ministry, Inc., https://OpenDoorToledo.org.

stairs for her." In her bag were eight rolls of toilet paper. Truly, this was the widow who gave her mite.

> *A poor widow came and put in two small coins, worth a few cents.*
> *Calling his disciples to himself, he said to them, "Amen, I say to you, this poor widow put more than all contributors to the treasury. For they all contributed from their surplus wealth, but she, from her poverty, has contributed all she had, her whole livelihood."*
> *(Mark 12:42–44)*

Two days later, a passerby noticed smoke coming out of the basement window of the house. He knew that this was a ministry for the homeless and called the fire department. One of the residents had set two rolls of toilet paper on fire in the basement. Once again, God's protection was upon us!

Many homeless came to the door when they were dying. We would make every effort to find out their names and any family that might be identified. In one case, an elderly man, who would forever be nameless since he was not known to anyone in the community, came seeking shelter in his illness. The Little Sisters of the Poor took him in, cared for him, and buried him in the end.

One of the local hospitals dropped a man off on the front lawn of the Open Door, who had his leg in a cast. The hospital said he had a habit of throwing himself in front of cars and would sell his crutches, wheelchairs, and walkers for his personal gain. They were very frustrated as to how to care for him. He told them to take him to the Open Door. It was always with love and welcome that our residents were cared for. This angry man met with this love, and after several months of care, he became gentled in spirit.

In my mind, the most beautiful story of God's love and care for the least of our brothers was our dear Henry. Henry was a genteel Southern gentleman, who was found sleeping on a city bench in the middle of winter, following his being released from the hospital after open-heart surgery. Henry was brought to the Open Door and remained with us for a year. He became a father figure to so many of the younger men. He loved it when I came by with my baby daughter, so he could hold her and talk to her. He always gave me suggestions on child care.

One day, Henry announced that he had to leave the house since he had broken the house rules and was off his meds and drinking. He said he could no longer be an example to the other men in the house. Henry disappeared from the community. One day, several months later, the Lord laid on my heart that I had to find Henry. I went to daily Mass and wanted to find Jeff, our resident director, to ask him to come with me to some of the places I did not want to visit alone. When I asked Jeff what he was doing that day, he responded that he was going to look for Henry. We knew beyond a doubt that God was sending us on a mission. We bought some of Henry's favorite things—a submarine sandwich, toiletries, new clean socks, and shoe polish. After searching the docks, farmer's market, and several hotels, we found the place where he was staying. When we knocked on his door, Henry opened it and fell to his knees, crying. He said, "Today is my birthday, and I prayed that if there was a God in heaven, then he should show me one person who knew me and cared about me. He not only sent one, but he sent you two."

Truly this was the gospel:

> *Look at the birds in the sky; they neither sow nor reap, they gather nothing into barns, yet your heavenly father feeds them. Are you not of more important than they. (Matthew 6:26)*

> *Are not two sparrows sold for a small coin? Yet not one of them falls to the ground without your Father's knowledge. (Matthew 10:29)*

This ministry is blessed to have been in existence for forty years. It has grown under the leadership and guidance of so many, who have maintained the vision and encouraged its growth to numerous facilities. Hundreds of homeless have been rehabilitated through this ministry. It is just one example of what God can do with the simple "yes" to his call. If he could use me, he could use anyone.

Reflection:

- How do you view the homeless?
- What ministries can you identify that serve those less fortunate?
- Familiarize yourself with "Seven Themes of Catholic Social Teaching," *United States Conference of Catholic Bishops*, Washington DC, 2005.

CHAPTER 7
The Life of a Child

At the age of thirty-seven, I had two sons, ten years old and seven years old. After my son Kevin was born, I could not move my arms without difficulty and extreme pain. I did not realize at the time that I suffered from congenital spinal stenosis that had been aggravated by my labor. From that point on, I chose to end my childbearing. I was aware that artificial birth control was a serious sin in Catholic teaching, yet I felt that it was a matter of conscience that I committed this sin.

However, one day in prayer, I heard the Lord say, "*I ask you to have another child. What are you afraid of? Are you afraid to sacrifice the career you love? Look at the sacrifice I asked of Abraham. Are you afraid you will not have patience? Look at the patience I asked of Job. What if I told you that your daughter would be gentle and loving and gather many to me?*"

I realized then that I would be limiting God's hand in bringing forth goodness for the next generation. Therefore, my beautiful faith-filled husband and I agreed to God's providence. I did not realize I was pregnant because I was so preoccupied with my life. That would change when I attended a healing service in our diocese and an obstetrician, with a prophetic gift, came up to me and told me that I was pregnant and I did not know it. He invited me to come to his office for an ultrasound if I did not believe him. I was confronted with the truth. The baby was due near the end of July. Later in my pregnancy, a priest prayed over me and said that God wanted me to know that my daughter would be born on June 21. On June 20, as my husband and I were exiting a birthing class there was a rainbow in the sky. Taking this as a sign from God, I immediately went home and packed my suitcase. Our Mary Kathryn was born the next day! She was 4 lbs. 13 oz. when we brought home our feisty daughter.

No, our lives are not predestined for us. We have a choice—to follow God's will, choose our own path through life, or choose the path of sin. Katie chose to follow God's will for her life and has been a youth minister in the Baptist Church for over twenty years. She and her husband have always led large youth groups, both in college and in their church, and hundreds of young people have been encouraged to grow in faith through their ministry. Their four children are the delights and treasures of our lives today. I chuckle when the boys, at the age of three and five years old, bring out their guitars and make me stand to pray while they "lead worship" from the living room hearth. All four of their children are extremely faith-filled, intelligent, and kind. They are a true measure of the good that God has placed in our world.

God was not quite finished with our childbearing. After our Katie was born, the Lord asked us to come to him in faith. We were now following the Church's teaching on natural family planning. I was therefore very surprised to find myself pregnant for the fourth time. This time, I heard the Lord say, *"To me, a child is more precious a gift than gold, frankincense, and myrrh."* We named our fourth child Ryan Matthew, which means royal gift from God. Because of the reference to the gifts presented to Jesus by the Magi at his birth, I took this as a sign that Ryan might be born on the Feast of the Epiphany, January 6, which was very close to his due date of January 20. I was surprised when I went into labor on December 28. Nonetheless, the Lord showed me his hand when I lost all of my gold jewelry in the hospital. It was either stolen out of my drawer while I was in the labor room or while I was sleeping. In my anger, the Lord reminded me, *"A child is more precious a gift than gold."*

I was at a Mass several months later when a woman came up to me to ask for healing prayer. She had miscarried several babies and wanted prayer for her current pregnancy. After praying for her, she insisted that I take the gold cross she was offering to me so that I would remember to pray for her. The more that I resisted this offer, the more she insisted to *please* take it. I relented and later asked the Lord's forgiveness for accepting a gift for the grace he had given to me. He responded, *"What mother would not exchange her gold for the health of her child? I tell you that a time will come in my Holy Mother the Church when she will exchange her gold for the health of the children. Pray, pray always!"* (June 1985).

I believe that this was the Lord's prophecy for the answer to the terrible scandal that has fallen upon our church in recent years. I have witnessed a newly assigned archbishop come into our diocese after the church's suffering from previous scandals. He had to sell off major properties, and church assets, and close churches and schools to pay for legal fees for those who were abused by our priests.

I am reminded of the dream of the ark when the masts and sails were torn down and the bare ark remained, lifted high above the seas with a rainbow in the sky. We as the church will be safe in her foundation. We may look different in the future, but we will never be destroyed for we are forever fortified by our rootedness in Christ.

Upon further reflection, I believe that the church has a prophetic role in the world, a knowledge that includes the continuum of time. With the introduction into society of artificial birth control, promiscuity, and violence against women that has grown at an alarming rate, the fabric of the family is being destroyed. Fewer children are being born, limiting God's hand to the good that he wants to bring into the world. We have allowed gender transformation in young children, who will forever be confused as to their true identity before God. The Chinese government condemned a whole society by limiting a couple to one child, resulting in skewed gender proportions and greater violence within the male population. Perhaps the wisdom born in the church is a foreknowledge of a greater evil that could come upon us. Our children are a gift from God and our gift to God.

Reflection:

- Reflect on the "Regulations of Births" in *Humanae Vitae: Encyclical Letter of His Holiness Pope Paul VI* (Ignatius Press, 1983).
- Journal how you see your role in the continuum of time. Do you pray for God to show you how he wants to use you?

CHAPTER 8

The Environment

Growing up in a regional area surrounded by refineries and chemical companies, perhaps it was a natural progression for most of my family to become scientists. From an early age, I was fascinated by nature and found that I had a natural aptitude for the sciences. I attended Rutgers University NCAS and majored in chemistry. Upon graduation, I was employed as a pesticide chemist at a large agricultural research center for a major manufacturer. I suppose it was providential that when I got married and moved to Washington DC, I would find myself employed at the Food and Drug Administration in their pesticide division. I did not willingly seek out this focused pesticide science.

For my research project at the FDA, I was introduced to a ton of fish that had an unknown substance interfering with the analysis of the pesticide DDT and its analogs. I was charged to identify and determine how to separate these unknown substances from the pesticides so the integrity of the pesticide analysis was not compromised when measuring them in foods.

I was able to determine that the substances contained in the fish were PCBs[3], better known as polychlorinated biphenyls. These are plasticizers with thousands of uses. They had entered our environment and migrated up the food chain to find their presence in mammals

---

[3]   Scholarly articles by J. Armour on PCB. Google.com.

and even in mother's milk. It was soon determined that these were a global pollutant. Every effort from that point on was to work diligently, within the United States government and with foreign entities, to eradicate them from further use and casual discard. I know, beyond a doubt, that God's gift of knowledge led me every step of the way to this profound discovery.

I was awestruck to see how easily this toxin could impact our environment and migrate through the food chain to spread throughout the globe. The Lord would remind us:

> *God created man in his image; in the divine image he created him; male and female he created them. God blessed them saying: "Be fertile and multiply; fill the earth and subdue it. Have dominion over the fish of the sea, the birds of the air, and all living things that move on the earth.* (Genesis 1:27–28)

Today, we as consumers have grown far from the simplicities of the lives of our forefathers. We do not pay enough attention to how our neglect and our waste impact our environment. We live in an interrelationship of a great design to life in our universe, programmed from the first atoms, by our loving God. The miracle of the order of the universe and our very bodies are not an accidental design. They demonstrate an amazing wonder, beyond our imaginings, by a God who is! If we allow disorder to reign according to man's impulses, we will fall out of balance and into a cataclysm that will lead to our own demise.

Reflection:

- What can I do to become more mindful of my environment?
- Read: Francis. 2015. *Encyclical Letter Lautio Si' of the Holy Father Francis*. 1st ed. Vatican City. (Retrieved from the Vatican website).

CHAPTER 9

Bearing the Cross

Every Lent, I ask the Lord to show me my sin. It is the perennial chastisement to see that pride is an ever-present obstacle for me. As much as I try to work on this root of my sins, the more I am faced by my human frailties. There were times when I let the awareness of these sins enter my conscience, and I would have to deal with them head-on. What was in darkness would now come into the light.

After I had given birth to my daughter Katie, I had to hand over the leadership of the healing retreats to the healing team. Renee led the group on one particular weekend retreat; however, we had a new priest as our spiritual director who had never been involved with a healing retreat before. Somewhere in the course of the weekend, several problems arose that were concerning to the team. They called me to come so that they would have more discernment. The Mercy Sisters said they would help look after the baby while I was on-site at their Mother House. The problems were quickly resolved. Later in the evening, it came time for the retreatants and team to be prayed over. When my turn arrived, I laughingly asked for the gift of bilocation (See what I mean by the lack of humility?). This would allow for me to be in two places at once—home with the children and at the retreat house with the team. Needless to say, I was surprised to hear the Lord say, "*I give you this gift. For while you will be physically removed from this place, you will remain behind in spirit.*"

Two weeks later, the Fortune 500 company, by which my husband was employed, was in the throes of a hostile takeover, and the company had to divest much of its holdings. This would directly impact my husband. He was charged with having to outplace his entire division, either within what was to be left of the company or to get them counseling for career change outside of the company. He would be unemployed at the end of this time. Obviously, this would have a great impact on our family and my ministries. What I learned was that the role of the prophet is to bring forth the vision and then to enable others to carry it on. It is letting go!

I had to prepare the way for the Open Door to be placed in the hands of the board of directors. This created a great sadness for me because I would miss seeing the beauty of God's presence in this ministry. However, being in charge of this ministry to the homeless was analogous to running another household, having another career, and heading a social agency. With the constant worry over the finances for the ministry, I could not and would not allow it to expand. It took new energy and vision to change the dynamics of the operation and to allow the ministry to grow. It is now forty years later, and the growth and success of the Open Door Ministry is beyond what I could have envisioned. Truly, God led forth others, whom he graced with gifts and talents far greater than my own.

The same was true of the healing ministry. It, too, expanded to the far reaches of the diocese. Our healing team, as previously noted, continued to serve the church across the country in a variety of roles.

One of the things I often witnessed in regard to those in church ministry is the reluctance to let go of their leadership. There is a tendency to take ownership of these ministries. This in turn becomes a stumbling block to growth. If we are to continue the discipleship that God calls us to, we must become enablers, who call forth the gifts of others. It is our responsibility to step back and step away from where we have served, trusting that God will raise up others with gifts greater than our own. I loved one of my husband's responses to a coworker who asked him about his recent promotion. Jim was always considered a beloved leader, who mentored and taught his employees all he knew about the businesses he ran. He responded, "If you are not dispensable, you are not promotable." So it is with God:

Anyone who is trustworthy in the little things is trustworthy in great; anyone who is dishonest in the little things, is dishonest in the great. (Luke 16:10)

There is a certain amount of dying to self that is required to admit that someone may be more gifted than you and better able to do your job. Trust that if the Lord wants something done, he will have his way and call forth another. Too often, I have seen ministries die because the old guard would not raise up others; they became complacent in their roles and redundant in their agendas. If true growth is to take place, we need to move over.

My family was later moved to Lancaster, Pennsylvania. I was now closer to my aging family who lived in New Jersey and New York State. I knew I would have to take on added responsibilities, and the dynamics of my life would change. Although I loved my mother, we never fostered a close relationship. We shared very little dialogue throughout my life; therefore, I knew that this was an area of my life that I had to work on.

Every year, my family had two weeks of vacation. We would spend one week with my family and one week with my husband's family. The week with my family resulted in my mother spending all of her time cooking and cleaning in her kitchen. My sister and I decided to resolve this issue by planning a vacation at a rented beach house so we could change the dynamics of the week we spent together. Now that my mother did not have meals to prepare or to endlessly clean, she took on a new task of bringing a year's worth of coupons to the beach. Every day, she would sit there clipping coupons and asking us if we used certain items. This distraction from reading a book, playing games with the kids, or just watching TV nearly put me over the edge of my patience.

When I mentioned this to my spiritual director the day before I was to leave on vacation, Father Sam said that he was bringing me a bon voyage gift that I could not open until after he left. Later in that day, Father came to my house with a small, neatly wrapped package. When I opened it, it was a pair of scissors with a note that said, "Help clip the coupons." True to form, the second night that we were sitting down to relax, out came the coupons. Being obedient to my spiritual director, I sat down to help clip coupons and discussed what I did and did not use due to my likes and dislikes. My mother put the coupons away that night, and I never saw them again for the entire trip. Upon reflection, I realized that this was my mother's way of trying to communicate. I also came to understand the family dynamics that she grew up with. My grandmother was orphaned at a very young age. She had no mother to model herself after; her life had a loving void and was based on survival. She in turn raised my mother with the very same instincts and lack of nurturing. When I came to this understanding, our relationship grew closer. I could finally say to Father Sam, "If anything happens to my mother, I think I can now serve her in love, instead of a sense of duty."

It was six months later that my father had a heart attack and needed open-heart surgery. My mother had spinal surgery and spiraled into dementia, later diagnosed as Alzheimer's disease. Jim had been offered a promotion to a position in California, which would cause us to move three thousand miles away from my ailing family, plus Jim's father was also in the beginning stages of dementia. When Jim turned down this offer, he found himself unemployed for the next year and a half. We had two sons in high school and our two younger children in grade school. I had to leave at all hours of the day and night to travel two and a half hours to help my father with my mother's latest crisis. It became obvious that I needed to move my parents into our home. While dealing with the ongoing care of two parents with enormous medical needs, I, too, began to have grave health problems. In one year, I would require three surgeries, spinal surgery on my neck, a stage three melanoma, and gallbladder surgery.

I remember dreaming about a girl who was hemorrhaging. When I took it to prayer, I knew that I was the girl who was hemorrhaging as my energies were being taxed. I asked the Lord to help me through the crisis that was my life. As I washed my mother, I was led to realize that I was washing the feet of Christ. When my mother left the house and I feared that she was lost in the dense woods, it was like Christ finding the lost sheep. I rejoiced when we located her. When my sons signed our family up to bring Our Lady of Fatima statue into our home, along with the Marian group of women who would accompany her, I gave them the responsibility of providing refreshments and leading the prayer. I was heartened to see that they relied on their faith to seek answers for the chaos that was present in our lives. I quickly learned to triage our responsibilities. We all had to find faith, love, and humor to get through those days.

Two years later, my husband found employment that would once again cause us a major move. This time, we had two sons in college, my mother in the end stages of Alzheimer's, and my father seriously ill. I was looking for nursing homes for my mother in two states, not knowing where we should be. I knew that only total surrender to God's will would guide us through these times.

We were looking for a house we could afford that would accommodate our expanded family. We also needed a school system that had programs for special education that would serve the needs of our youngest son. After months of searching, I found an exceptional nursing home for my mother. After taking a wrong turn upon leaving the nursing home, I found a beautiful neighborhood. It was outside of the school system where we were concentrating our search, but I found a school near the neighborhood and decided to stop in and make inquiries about the services they provided for special education. The principal welcomed me as I gained entry into his office. He was dressed as a huge teddy bear. When I told him what I wanted to know, he said to wait and he would change out of his very special look and agreed to show me around.

The school had state-of-the-art accommodations for handicapped children, complete with ramping throughout the school for wheelchair access. Every classroom had special reading booths for individualized instructions. The school focused on the affirmation of all students. He then introduced me to the special education instructor, who had her PhD in Special Education and later revealed to me that she had been a Carmelite nun for seven years. For me, this was the stamp that God had provided to guide us to where we should be.

Later, we found a house that we loved but couldn't afford, two miles from the nursing home and the school. The home was vacant and very contemporary for the historic nature of the community. We therefore felt justified to put in a ridiculously low offer on the house that was the limit of what we could afford. Neither Jim nor I could remember much about the house since we wouldn't allow ourselves to fall completely in love with it. We were later ecstatic to find out that our offer was accepted. We laughingly needed to revisit the house to see what we had just bought. As we looked in the window of the main living area, stenciled on the wall in front of us was a five-foot, sunlit ichthys, the fish that was the ancient sign for Christ. This sign could never be explained although, for many years, it would appear near the end of every May on that same spot.

We moved into this home, and my mother died three months later. My father would live with us for another four years before he, too, passed away. We moved in my mother-in-law, whom we cared for until her death. Several years later, my niece moved in with us, and we were blessed to have her and three of our children married from this house of blessing! This is a foretelling of how we pass from death to resurrection in our lives.

The Easter Tridium is always a special time of retreat for me. It is a profound time for prayer and reflection as I kneel before the cross in humble reverence. One Good Friday, I was in meditation on the readings when the Lord said to me, *"Accept the garment that I was stripped of as your mantle for you are a prophet. I call you by another name; it is Mary Petrina. Mary for my mother whom I have gifted you with throughout your life, and Petrina, the Russian derivative of Peter. You, like Peter, are strong and obstinate and eventually obedient to do my will. Your ministry will not end until you reach Russia."*

My response was, "Then Lord, let this mantle be my shroud."

Years later, I heard the Lord say, *"I tell you that you must now bear the cross."*

I know this would bring about another disruption in my life, and my response was, "Really, Lord, is there no other way?"

He said, *"While your flesh is weak, your soul has vanquished that response."*

I soon became more and more debilitated as I was having trouble getting out of a chair and walking. I was losing the use of my arms. A neurosurgeon at one of the top spine centers in the country said that I needed extensive surgery on my cervical spine; this was not an optional surgery but a necessary one since my spinal cord was a mere thread. A simple fall would leave me completely paralyzed. I therefore agreed to have my surgeon present my case at the Neurosurgeons East Coast Conference in order to get input on how to progress with the surgery. I understand that they came to the consensus that all of the lamina in my cervical spine should be removed and replaced by rods and screws. If the neuro signals to my feet increased, more extensive surgery could be avoided. This eighteen-hour surgery was a success, but I was in horrific pain when I came home. It was difficult to move even a finger without excruciating pain. When the nurse and physical therapist came to the house, they realized that something was decidedly wrong. It required that I return to the hospital in a snowstorm to find out that I had not been given the correct pain medication. Also, the internal stitches had ruptured and were poking through my skin. Recovery was slow but successful.

Following my recovery, we found out that the company that Jim was president of was compromised by the parent company, and once again, he was out of a job. He was unemployed for two years, and we still had children in college. Our health care was ending, and we had to resort to drastic measures to stay solvent. I was on a retreat when one of the women in the group mentioned how much she loved her job at Immaculata University. I knew I had to look for employment so we could have our family covered by medical insurance. The first place I sought out was the university this woman mentioned. I found an academic counseling position that had just become open. With no previous experience in this career, I still decided to apply. I knew that I could use my leadership skills and intellect to adapt to new environments. Imagine my surprise when I was offered the position and came to learn that I was replacing the woman I met on retreat. She was being promoted to another position. Once again, this was a cross that ended with a resurrection.

The greatest cross I would come to bear is that of having to bury a child. It was always my greatest fear and one the devil used when wanting to tempt me during a release prayer where evil was present in the person's life.

Jim and I were vacationing in Florida at the home of Renee (my sister in faith) and her husband David when we got the call from our son Kevin, telling us that our oldest son Patrick was in a medical crisis and he was being transferred from a hospital in Summit County, Colorado, to a major medical center in Denver due to an esophageal rupture. Our son Kevin was flying out on the next flight to be with him since neither Jim nor I could breathe at the high altitude. Providentially, we were having a prayer group meeting that night at Renee and David's house that included people we knew from our ministry back in Toledo.

As we prayed, I received the prophecy: *"On the day you gave birth to your son on earth, I will bring him to New Birth and New*

Life in Heaven. " I knew then that Patrick would die the next day, on his birthday, which was February 25. For everyone who had died in my presence, I was praying a rosary as they passed. I therefore was praying one for Patrick when he passed from death to life. Kevin said that Patrick's good friend, who had followed the ambulance to Denver, called for a priest to be with Patrick, and she was praying the rosary when Kevin arrived. As Kevin was closing the door to Patrick's room in his apartment for the last time, he noticed that the sunlight was reflecting off something shiny hanging from the lamp. It was Patrick's first communion medal and a rosary.

I believe in God winks—"the heavenly signs our loved ones send to help our hearts to slowly mend." Several weeks after Patrick's death, we noticed so many yellow butterflies outside on our deck. One flew into Jim's face. I looked online to see what kind of butterfly they were. They were called yellow clouds. Next to the posting was an addendum that stated that yellow butterflies represent new birth and new life.

We all face crosses sometimes in our lives; they are part of our human condition. They cause pain and suffering, but they also help us grow in strength and wisdom. When I think that my flesh is weak, I am reminded that the soul is greater than flesh and answers for us with a heavenly response. Our God is a good God who brings us through these times filled with his love for us. Let us look through the eyes of faith to see the kingdom of God that is ever-present. God never leaves us orphaned, and he guides our footsteps. Through him, there is no death but a passing to a greater life.

Reflection:

- Recall situations in your life when you had to surrender your will to God. How did God respond?
- If I am going through the stages of grief, am I angry at God, or do I seek him for consolation?

CHAPTER 10
My Life in the Church

There was never a time in my life that I questioned the existence of God nor lost my fervent love for the church. I remember my grandfather blessing me when I was still in my crib and teaching me to bless myself in Slovak. At the age of four, I was standing in the backyard and thinking that there must have been a time of a great void when only God existed. What did he have in mind when he created the world and all that is in it? All I ever felt from God was love. I believed that our church was an extension of that love.

In my childhood, we belonged to a very progressive church in Roselle Park, New Jersey. The 9:00 a.m. Mass was the children's Mass. Prior to Vatican II, we would be led by the nuns to read the prayer responses within the Mass in English. After our confirmation at the age of twelve, we spent the remaining years of junior high and high school studying the Scripture, led by our associate pastor who was a scripture scholar. This was the beginning of my love for the Scripture.

When I first got married, my husband served as an officer in the military. While stationed in Korea, I joined him for six weeks. We traveled throughout Asia for a month and returned to the base for the remaining two weeks. The priest on base asked if I would reach out to the women in the small town, just outside of the base, to help them understand American customs and introduce them to feminine hygiene. Some of these women were in a relationship with young soldiers and close to being married to them. He explained that many of the women had been sold off by their families and were not educated. This priest had great compassion for the people he served. The time I spent with these women was truly a mission for me. I still hold those women close to my heart. It was here that I first got to experience the universal church.

When I was in my early thirties, I recall being at the last Mass that our pastor and our associate pastors would celebrate before they left our parish for retirement and other assignments respectively. I prayed that God would send us someone who would bring life into the parish. It was the first time I heard the Lord speak. I was reminded of the gospel passage *"why do you notice the splinter in your brother's eye, but do not perceive the wooden beam in your own eye?"* (Matthew 7:3).

I knew I was convicted and thought that I needed to be doing something in the parish. I said to the Lord that I would do whatever he needed me to do. Imagine my surprise when I stepped out of the side door of the church and there was Sister Maria Goretti. She grabbed my arm and said, "You are just the person that I am looking for. Would you be interested in heading up the preschool program for religious education?" I think I startled her with my immediate "yes." She told me that I would have to attend classes to become certified through the diocese. Again, I startled her by saying, "I would do whatever was necessary." This was the beginning of my ministry in the church.

My time spent in the Toledo Ohio Diocese came shortly after Vatican II. The changes in the church were being fully embraced. The laity were encouraged to serve the church and to take on leadership roles. Here, I became certified as a catechist, a spiritual director, and an evangelist. Under the guidance and authority of the priests and bishop, my husband and I served in many varied ministries. When I shared with my pastor how God was revealing himself to me, I was not met with doubt. Father said, "I know you and the fruits of your life, I believe that this is a true religious experience. You need greater direction than what I can give you." He then suggested I meet with Father Carl Recker, who was the liaison to the bishop for the Charismatic Renewal, and with Father James Bacik, a mystical theologian. Without the direction of these priests and that of Bishop James Hoffman, the many miracles that were witnessed through the healing ministry and the ministry to the homeless would not have occurred.

Bishop Hoffman gave me a letter of introduction to the Harrisburg, Pennsylvania diocese when I moved. I was immediately embraced by the Pastor, Father William Sullivan, of my new parish. He told me that the first of its kind, Leadership in Ministry Program, was starting up in the diocese and that he would like for me to attend. It would be a huge commitment on my part since it was three years of formation that required meeting every week plus one weekend a month of meeting, both locally and in Harrisburg. He had already selected the fifteen from our parish who agreed to attend; however, he would add me to the roster if I would like to participate. What he failed to mention was that we would be given assignments at the end of the program at the discretion of the pastor. To my surprise, he asked me to become the youth minister. At the age of forty-four, I felt like Jeremiah the prophet, who claimed he was too young. I on the other hand felt that I was too old. I told Father that I would go on a silent retreat for a weekend and pray about it. I should have reminded myself that if you are so heavenly bound, you are no earthly good.

However, I met the Lord at every turn during the retreat. He reminded me that the youth were living stones called to build the kingdom of God on earth. I dreamed about hungry teenagers to whom I wanted to feed fish, but when I dove in the water, instead of fish, I found eggs. When we broke the eggs open, they were filled with gemstones. Again, I was being given gems (Revelations 21:19–20)—a sign of divine creation. Later in the day, while walking in the garden of this beautiful retreat center in Wernersville, Pennsylvania, a duck flew up so close to my face that I felt the breath of its wings as it startled me. When I stooped down to see where it came from, there was a nest full of eggs. I returned to my parish and agreed to serve as the youth minister, which I did for the next five years.

The Leadership in Ministry Program was also a precursor for men who were discerning their call to the diaconate. Along with these men were a group of Women Religious, who had left their religious orders of sisters; however, they maintained their religious vows. Under the tutelage of Archbishop William H. Keeler, these sisters were being formed into a new paradigm of religious life. They were to become Diocesan Sisters, who would live independently and be assigned to specific parishes, universities, and medical facilities, rather than live in a community. Archbishop Keeler wanted these nuns to pray weekly with each other and with select lay women. I was fortunate to have been asked to be part of this prayer group.

Before this order could gain canonical status, Archbishop Keeler was transferred to Baltimore, where he would be raised up to become a Cardinal. He offered to bring these sisters along to Baltimore with him to continue their formation. However, they were too immersed in their roles and did not feel it was the right time to leave those commitments. Many of these sisters later joined the Society of Sisters for the Church based in Paterson, New Jersey.

Once again, I was about to leave another loving community and move outside of the diocese. My pastor said he was sorry that I had to move to the Philadelphia diocese since they were slow to embrace Vatican II and had not empowered the laity. He reminded me to be patient.

At the beginning of my spiritual journey, when the Lord placed the mantel of the prophet upon me in a meditation and called me by my other name, he also said, "*A time will come when they will bind you with a girdle and sever your hands. Know then that you do not need your hands to pray, merely make the command in my name; and it will be done.*" Since I had prayed that this mantel become my shroud, I took this prophecy to have a more ominous meaning. This personal prophecy would play out in many different ways. The first of the serious symptoms of my compromised spinal cord was that I had extreme pain in my arms and hands, followed by losing feeling in my hands. I was dropping things at an alarming rate.

However, metaphorically, my hands have been bound from doing God's work with the same freedom I had in my two previous dioceses when I moved to the Philadelphia diocese over twenty-eight years ago.

When I arrived in my new parish, I presented myself to the director of Religious Education and asked if she could use someone to serve in the youth ministry. Sister told me that there was no youth ministry in the parish, and I quote her response, "Catechetics are not fun and games." The twenty-five years that I served as a catechist were scoffed at since I never attended Catholic School.

With two preteens, I was disheartened to find out that they would have no further Catholic formation in the church beyond their Confirmation unless I sent them to a Catholic High School. This was not an option because my son would not get the additional specialized help that he needed for his learning disability in the local Catholic High School. After some research, I learned that there was a Christian ministry for youth in the community called Young Life. This ecumenical group was national, had a terrific reputation for bringing teens to Christ and helping them to grow in their discipleship. Both of my teens joined this group and found that many of their Catholic friends from their school and from our parish were also participating. Jim and I joined the adult board of this wonderful organization to make sure that they were not proselytizing our youth. To the contrary, they provided them with books about being Catholic and Christian and brought them to Mass when they were on retreat or at camps. My daughter, who the Lord promised would be *"gentle and loving, and gather many to him,"* grew in faith and Christian leadership. She received her master's degree in counseling and has been a youth minister in the Baptist Church for over twenty years. She and her husband have led hundreds of youths to Christ.

I was saddened that my own parish could not provide this same opportunity for my children. I learned that there was a Catholic

Leadership Program that had been formed within our cluster of parishes for teens who attended public schools. I told my pastor about this program and asked if I could take on the responsibility of including our parish in the program. He agreed to it somewhat reluctantly. He told me to do it clandestinely through the rectory and not to let the director of Religious Education know what I was doing. I carried out this role for the four remaining years that my children were in high school. I also inquired about joining a Bible study when we first moved into the parish. I was told that it was already full. I realized that if I wanted to find fellowship, I could have joined the Women's Group and helped with craft fairs and bake sales. To say I have no artistic ability would be an understatement.

I quickly learned that a prophet is without honor in their home. I therefore continued to serve outside of my diocese. I led retreats, provided spiritual direction, spoke at conferences, and headed leadership formation for church ministry when invited to do so. Within my own parish, I lived in the shadows. I encouraged the men, who led the committees I sat on, to bring forth new programs for evangelization. I aligned myself with other diocesan initiatives, where I participated in the pilot program for interfaith dialogue. I could not abandon the homeless, and I found that I could cook for them and serve them in a neighboring parish's soup kitchen.

I attended a talk several years ago that the Philadelphia diocese presented on the role of women in the church. A woman religious, who was a theologian, gave a talk on the various definitions of gender identity. She summed up the talk with the consensus that women could never be ordained since their primary role within the church was to procreate. At the conclusion of her presentation, my temples were throbbing, my heart was racing, and I realized that if someone spoke in tongues, I had an interpretation. These physical manifestations were, for me, the sign that God had something to say, and it was to be so specific that I could not know what it was that I was to speak until I began to utter the first words. Obviously, no one would speak in tongues in this setting. Instead, I found my hand shooting up immediately when the question and answers portion of the program started. I was led to ask, *"Since there is a biblical reference to women as deacons in the church, why aren't our Women Religious being considered for ordination to the deaconate? They have denied their procreative role through their vows of chastity, and many have master's degrees and PhDs in theology."* I immediately received a tap on my shoulder from an auxiliary bishop who was sitting behind me. He said that was a great question and one that should be entered into the discussion.

I was reminded of a time when our parish was asked to pray for our deacons in formation. I heard the Lord say, *"Why are you praying for them when it is you that I call."* I realized that I had indeed served my church in so many roles and that I did not need to be ordained to continue. However, I believe the diaconate could be a new paradigm for Women Religious.

I am old, and I will soon turn seventy-seven, and just when I think the Lord is done with me, he asks one more thing. I received an invitation from the Raleigh, North Carolina diocese to participate in the Synod Discussion for Discerning Women as Deacons.[4] I received two emails, and I ignored them. When I received the third email, I prayed and determined that I could not deny the Lord three times. I registered for the discussion and participated in the international Zoom meeting. I was humbled by the amazing work that women all over the world are doing for our church. In South America, one woman religious was traveling to over sixty parishes, performing baptisms and weddings due to the lack of priests. I remember many years ago, learning that women in some European churches were performing para liturgies and bringing the precious consecrated hosts from a central parish to churches where there were not enough priests to serve.

Remembering the Women Religious I prayed with back in Harrisburg and the many Women Religious that I have served with over the years, I can think of no better paradigm for their orders to

---

4   Discerning Deacons, https://discerningdeacons.org.

survive than to ordain them as deacons.

I disavow myself from any feminist or woke agenda in making this plea. I am the woman who was placed with twenty-eight males and one other female in all of my high school classes since I was following a college curriculum for math and science. I would enter a predominately male chemistry major in college, where my professors encouraged me to not choose to become a teacher but to follow a research tract through to graduation. While working for the Food and Drug Administration in Washington DC, Elliott Richardson, then Secretary of Health Education and Welfare, asked me to sit on a task force for discussions about equal opportunity for minorities. I paused to think which minority he expected me to represent.

I never considered myself oppressed in any way because of my gender. However, when the pastor in my confession told me that I had to get over the "male thing," which by the way had nothing to do with anything I confessed, I was taken aback. I can say, without reservation, that I have filled my role as a woman within the church. I have procreated by bringing four beautiful children into this world and raising them in faith. I have been a good daughter to my parents. I have served my God and his church faithfully and to the best of my ability. Our beautiful Blessed Mother has seen me through my sorrows and has been my strength and my model.

I have seen my church in three different stages of evolution. First, the church that empowered the laity; the second, a church that was now raising up the laity; and the third, a church that was afraid of the laity. This last was where my hands were severed!

Reflection:

- How would you describe your place in your life and/or the life of the church?

CHAPTER 11
The Covenant

I have friends, who are very faithful and traditional Catholics, who send me heretical YouTube postings and books they receive about the Vatican, Pope Francis, and the infiltration of the Vatican by evil for my discernment. The authors of these podcasts and books imply that recent popes were under the influence of Satan. Would these individuals deny that the conclave of cardinals who cast ballots for the selection of the pope had been misguided by the Holy Spirit? This is not possible! If this were true, we are giving too much credit to the evil one and not trusting Christ to lead his church. It is disturbing to think that this schism against the pope is present within our church, but I have heard these same arguments from others whom I respect. They fail to realize that our pontiff comes from a different culture and has seen the hardships of poverty and oppression. Stepping into the opulence of the Vatican exposes the contrast of Western culture versus that of Third World cultures. We must remember that the Catholic Church is a universal church that spans the globe and encompasses all cultures. If God could speak to my heart, how much more will he speak to his holy elect!

When one becomes rigid in their thinking and closed to a greater plan that God has in mind for us, we are denying the possibility of God uniting the whole of humanity into the kingdom of God—the

Holy City where all will be united in faith and will share in the common good. It is going to be a painful transition at best! It may take a cataclysmic occurrence, but it will come to be. I remember the prophecy that the Lord gave me: *"I call you to be an ambassador for the faith. I tell you that there is faith and holiness in many religions. No one will have to compromise what they believe, only build on it."*

My time in the Diocesan Interfaith Dialogue Task Force humbled me as I listened to the deep faith in God from those in other major religions. I questioned how could God love them less? I believe that Jesus instituted the Catholic Church and gave us the truth to pass on, but I also believe that God has an incredible plan to unite us through the Trinity, the indivisible God.

I recently viewed the YouTube presentation of Rabbi Felix Halpern[5] who had an "afterdeath" experience of heaven and came back as a converted Messianic Jew. He experienced being covered by the blood of Christ, which kept him from evil that had no power over him in death.

The Jewish people hold a special place in my heart; I celebrate the roots of our Christianity through the Judaism of Christ. In my teenage years, I grew up in a neighborhood surrounded by three synagogues, and many of my friends were Jewish. I attended several Jewish services when they had their Bar and Bat Mitzvahs. I attended special services for the martyrs of the Holocaust and enjoyed Seder meals with them. The Jewish people have sacrificed so much for their faith yet never compromised their belief in God! They recognize God's actions in their lives and seek to hear his voice. They faithfully hold on to the Old Covenant.

Throughout Asia, I visited monasteries where the monks prayed constantly, fasted and led austere lives of introspection, seeking truth. I question why God has not shown them the truth that is Christ. Perhaps

---

[5] Destiny Image (March 8, 2023), "Rabbi Dies and Visits Heaven's Throne Room! Listen to What He Saw," https:// youtube.com/watch?v=cL6YcN-2mJh8.

because their beliefs are so ingrained in their culture and based on a unifying good that God thought to leave them alone for now.

I attended many lectures on the tenets of the Muslim faith and witnessed the discipline of their prayer throughout my travels in the Middle East. As a professed Third Order Franciscan, I loved the writings of Saint Bonaventure, who described the encounter of Saint Francis of Assisi when he met with the Sultan al-Malik al-Kamil in Egypt in 1219, in the midst of the Crusades, to seek common understanding and peace. The sultan recognized the holiness of Francis. While this meeting did not bring about the lasting peace that Francis hoped for, it did result in the two spending several days together, seeking greater understanding and respect for each other's traditions and beliefs.

Just maybe, God likes the diversity of sounds ringing from around the world. I believe that God has a plan bigger than we can imagine. We need to trust in the Holy Spirit to unite us all and guide us into his kingdom.

Nostra aetate (from Latin "in our time") is the declaration of the relation of the church with non-Christian religions.[6] This is one of the sixteen final documents of the Second Vatican Council, promulgated by Pope Paul VI. It states, "As the Sacred Synod searches into the mystery of the Church, it remembers the bond that spiritually ties the people of the New Covenant to Abraham's stock."

There are schisms in our churches, in our government, and within our communities. Out of the schism will come the truth. Scripture tells us, *"But he knew what they were thinking and said to them, 'Every kingdom divided against itself will be laid waste, and no town or house divided against itself will stand'"* (Matthew 12:25).

We are the remnant who stand at the fray; we are called to pray for truth. We need to allow God to bring about his kingdom in his

---

6 Nostra Aetate (October 28, 1965), http://www.vatican. va/archive/hist_councils/ ii_vatican_council/documents/ vatii_decl_19651028_nostra-aetate_en.html.

time and in his way. We are living stones, who will become the foundation of God's Holy City, through our love, prayers, forgiveness, and charity toward all.

God will hear our prayer. *"He will lead us into the Ark, two by two; of every nation, every race and every creed."* As the storm causes the waters around us to crash and roil, we should never lose hope. We are God's remnant who will not be destroyed. We will be safe in the hull of the Ark, the foundation of faith, the one church. The seas will calm as the Master of all navigates this Ark. He will fulfill his promise to lead us all safely to the New Jerusalem, the kingdom of peace, the fullness of life, and into an all-consuming love. This is his Covenant.

Reflection:

- After reading this book, do you want to live in this Fourth Dimension—where you encounter the living Christ in our midst? Still your mind, open your heart, and listen.

GLOSSARY

Eucharist

It is Christ himself, the eternal high priest of the New Covenant, who, acting through the ministry of the priests, offers the Eucharistic sacrifice. And it is the same Christ really present under the species of bread and wine, who is the offering of the Eucharistic sacrifice.
(*Catechism of the Catholic Church* [*CCC*], second edition, 2009 [para. 1410])

Holy Orders

The risen Christ, by giving the Holy Spirit to the apostles, entrusted to them his power of sanctifying; they became the sacramental sign of Christ. By the power of this same Holy Spirit, they entrusted this power to their successors.
(*Catechism of the Catholic Church* [*CCC*], second edition, 2009 [para. 1087])

Reconciliation or the Sacrament of Penance

This sacrament reconciles us with the church. Sin damages and/ or even breaks fraternal communion. The Sacrament of Penance repairs and restores it. In this sense, it not only heals the one restored to ecclesial communion, but also has a revitalizing effect on the life of the Church.
(*Catechism of the Catholic Church* [*CCC*], second edition, 2009 [para. 1469])

Sacraments

There are seven sacrament of the Catholic Church, which, according to Catholic theology, were instituted by Jesus and entrusted to the church. Sacraments are visible rites seen as signs and efficacious channels of the grace of God to all those who receive them with the proper disposition. These sacraments are Baptism, Confirmation, Eucharist, Penance, the Anointing of the Sick, Matrimony, and Holy Orders.
("Seven Sacraments," *Wikipedia* 2023, usccb.org)

Synod

A local or provincial assembly of bishops and other church officials meeting to resolve questions of discipline or administration.
(Google: April 26, 2023)

REFERENCES

Linn, Dennis, SJ, and Matthew Linn, SJ. 1974. *Healing of Memories*. New York/Mahwah, NJ: Paulist Press.

Destiny Image. March 8, 2023. *Rabbi Dies and Visits Heaven's Throne Room! Listen to What He Saw*. https:// youtube.com/ watch?vcL6YcN2mJh8.

Discerning Deacons. https://discerningdeacons.org.

Francis. 2015. *Encyclical Letter Lautio Si' of the Holy Father Francis*. 1ˢᵗ ed. Vatican City. (Retrieved from the Vatican website).

Nostra Aetate (October 28, 1965) http://www.vatican.va/archive/ hist_councils/ii_vatican_council/documents/vatii_decl_ 19651028_nostra-aetate_en.html.

Open Door Ministry, Inc. https://OpenDoorToledo.org.

"Regulations of Births." *Humanae Vitae: Encyclical Letter of His Holiness Pope Paul VI*. Ignatius Press, 1983.

Scholarly articles on PCB by J. Armour. Google.com.

"Seven Themes of Catholic Social Teaching." *United States Conference of Catholic Bishops*. Washington DC, 2005.

Society of the Sisters for the Church. https://ssc-usa.org.

The New American Bible. 1986. Nashville: Catholic Bible Press, Nelson Publishers.

ABOUT THE AUTHOR

Judith Perrine Armour retired from academia. She received her degree in chemistry from Rutgers University NCAS. While employed by the Food and Drug Administration in Washington, DC, she authored several scientific journal articles for her research on PCBs as environmental pollutants, leading to new government and international regulations for continuing use and casual discard of these substances. She developed a curriculum for teaching genetics while employed at the Medical College of Ohio. Most importantly, she is the founder of the Open Door Ministry for the homeless in Toledo, Ohio.

Judith has served in the Catholic Church for over forty years, taking on roles in healing ministries, spiritual direction, evangelization initiatives, interfaith dialogue, retreat direction, and synod discussions.

She has been married to her high school sweetheart and companion on the journey for over fifty-five years. She is the mother of four children and grandmother to eight grandchildren. She resides in West Chester, Pennsylvania.